To Tony,

Best wishes,

John Scheibe

June 13, 2009

On the Road
with Jim Murray

BASEBALL AND THE SUMMER OF 79

JOHN SCHEIBE

ENCINO MEDIA GROUP

On The Road with Jim Murray: Baseball and the Summer of '79
Copyright © 2007 John Scheibe
Published by Encino Media Group

For further information, please contact:

jpscheibe@mac.com

Cover Illustration by Margaret K. Scheibe
Photographs property of John P. Scheibe

Book design by:
Arbor Books
www.arborbooks.com

Printed in the United States

On The Road with Jim Murray: Baseball and the Summer of '79
John Scheibe

1. Title 2. Author 3. Sports

LCCN: 2007901152

ISBN 10: 0-9793709-0-6
ISBN 13: 978-0-9793709-0-8

To Vicky, Maggie and Betsy

Also, a special thanks to Mal Florence, who was a sportswriter's sportswriter, and columnist Al Martinez for their encouragement.

Contents

Prologue

Jim Murray stood on the elevator platform outside the Rose Bowl press box and gazed across the Arroyo Seco, the scenic gorge in Pasadena, California, where the historic stadium sits. It was a beautiful Sunday morning. He could see the bright sunshine, the puffy white clouds that dotted the blue sky and the dust of snow powder on the peaks of the nearby San Gabriel Mountains.

Murray surveyed the wintry Southern California scene, then said, "If somebody had told me I'd be standing here at the Rose Bowl today, I would never have believed it."

It was Super Bowl XIV, January 20, 1980, to be played between the Los Angeles Rams and the Pittsburgh Steelers. Almost exactly a year earlier, at the Super Bowl in Miami, Florida, Murray suffered a detached retina at the horse races the day before the game. Jim said one minute he was looking at the green infield of Gulfstream Park and then, suddenly, the green turf turned into what looked like egg salad with red worms. He was taken to the hospital with a bloody eye and he underwent emergency surgery, but that and follow-up treatment to repair the retina by specialists in Los Angeles and Boston were unsuccessful.

Jim's other eye, the right one, wasn't much better. It had a cataract that his doctors were hesitant to remove because there

1

was a good chance that if they tried, that retina would come off too. The man who was named national sportswriter of the year thirteen times, his column syndicated in over 200 newspapers around the world, a national treasure to America's newspaper readers and the one whom Muhammad Ali once called "the greatest sportswriter of alllllll tiiiiimme" outside the Los Angeles Lakers' dressing room after a playoff game with the Seattle SuperSonics, couldn't see more than a couple of feet in front of him.

So, as he languished in an ever-darkening world at his home in Bel-Air, Murray figured that, at age 59, his career was over.

But editors at the *Los Angeles Times*, where Jim had been a columnist since 1961, had a plan. Worried that circulation would drop because of Murray's absence, they told him they would do whatever was necessary to get him writing again. He could write his column four days a week instead of the normal five. And someone, possibly from the sports staff, would help him write it. Gerry Murray, Jim's wife and the rock that he clung to during this difficult ordeal, urged him to give it a try, and he agreed to do it.

At first, Murray's secretary at the paper, Marilyn White, went to his house to help him, but she found the experience emotionally draining and time consuming. She was also the secretary for the managers of the business and metro sections, and those people needed her to assist them too. After about a week, she returned to the office.

Then Murray thought he could get one of his three sons to help their father. But most of the time they either worked, surfed the inviting waves of Santa Monica Bay or played guitars in rock bands. As Gerry put it, "They're out doing their thing."

Finally, Jim called sports editor Bill Shirley for help and word went out to the staff that someone would be assigned full-time to Murray.

I was the night desk assistant in the sports department. I had had the job for nearly eight years after working as a copyboy and police reporter for the paper's news department. Surprisingly, none of the writers and copy editors applied to help Murray, even after Chuck Garrity, the assistant sports editor, said, "Whoever gets to work with Murray is going to have a great job."

When no one from the staff stepped forward, Garrity recommended me. He knew I liked sports, especially golf, and that I lived just a few minutes by car from Jim's house. It was also the time of year when the only major sport in progress was baseball, so one of the prep sports reporters who needed summer work could cover my duties, which included answering the telephone and clipping and distributing the stories from the Associated Press and United Press International wire service machines.

After a couple of days of thinking over Garrity's idea, Shirley told me I'd be the one to work with Murray for the summer. I was thrilled yet apprehensive at the same time. I had never been around anyone who was blind for any length of time.

There was a blind man who worked as a transcription typist at the *Times*. His name was Mike Leon, and once he came into the sports department to listen to a Dodgers game on the radio. He needed help to get to the radio which was on the other side of the room, so I took him by the arm and, on the way, he ran into nearly every trash can in the sports department.

In a weird way I was the one who was handicapped. My inexperience would result in Jim suffering a severe leg injury at the Rams' training camp at Cal St. Fullerton. He gashed his leg on a rusty sprinkler that I should have seen. We would make a memorable trip to the World Series and cover the Super Bowl and NBA Finals. I learned more about the newspaper business in six months sitting next to him than I had in nearly 10 years at the *Times*. He would lecture me about writing and freely give me advice on personal matters, as a father would to a son.

We crossed paths with some of the biggest names in the world of sports and show business, from athletes and actors to journalists and team managers, coaches and owners. When we would travel by car to an assignment or have lunch at his favorite restaurant, we'd talk about anything and everything: sports, music, writing, newspapers, stories he had covered for the old *L.A. Examiner* in the

1940s, his work at *Time* magazine as its Hollywood correspondent and at *Sports Illustrated*, the people he had met.

During the months he was without his sight, I rarely heard Jim complain. There was no self-pity. Maybe growing up in the gut of the Great Depression had somehow prepared him for this. In the 1930s, in places like Hartford, Connecticut, where Murray spent his early years, some people had just one meal a day. Nothing was taken for granted. It was a challenge for Jim to write his column, but it was also his lifeboat. He was usually upbeat, especially when we got to the ballpark. We had our good times, and bad, but we got through them. I was his eyes, but he guided me. It began with a knock on his door on a summer day in July of 1979.

Chapter One

THE TOY DEPARTMENT

"Here comes Cuomo, here comes the throw!" yelled Bob Cuomo, one of the writers on the high school and junior college sports desk, as he raced from the business section into the sports department and slid, a perfect hook slide on the slick, red linoleum floor, straight into a bank of shiny, black, wooden storage cabinets. The crash woke up Cal Whorton, the day edition sports editor, who was dozing in a chair in the corner of the room. He jumped up and swore, "What the hell was that?" Cuomo smiled sheepishly, picked himself up and went back to his desk. "Pretty hard-knockin' slide," he said with a cocky grin.

It would be easy to say it was a different time, both for the newspaper business and for sports, especially baseball, but it really wasn't. Memory lane can be a crooked road and the passage of 27 years can make recollections hazy, but a study of old sports pages revealed that events of the new millennium had also happened in the 1970s. Terror and murder had interrupted the 1972 Olympic Games in Munich. After he won the Olympic decathlon in 1976 at Montreal, one of Bruce Jenner's endorsements put his All-American smile on Wheaties cereal boxes. In baseball, free

5

agency and expansion had made indelible marks on the game, along with the tentacle-like influence of television and its new baby, cable TV. World Series and All-Star games were played at night. In the 1970s, the average salary of a big league player was $113,000; minimum pay was $21,000—both large sums for that era. Pitcher Jim "Catfish" Hunter was the game's highest-paid player. The New York Yankees had signed the former Oakland Athletics star for four years for what was called an "astounding" $2.85 million.

At the *Los Angeles Times* where I worked as a night desk assistant in the sports department, we used pencils, glue, ink-carbon paper and typewriters to produce an award-winning section—what some called not just the best in the country, but in the world. There were no laptops and cell phones. But we did have a bulky computer in the office that helped us send stories and scores straight to the linotypists in the composing room. And pagers were around; we called them "beepers." Championship fights were on pay-per-view television, but they were shown in theaters and basketball arenas. The downside was if fans arrived late and there was a knockout in the first round, there was no replay.

Players and teams had nicknames such as Yaz and Mr. October, Tom Terrific and the Big Red Machine, Dr. J and Magic.

I started at the *Times* as a copyboy in 1968, a shy and impressionable 20-year-old college student. I had come from a newspaper family. My mother, Donna, was a "society" reporter for the *Van Nuys News and Green Sheet* in the early 1960s. Later, she went to the *Times* as a news reporter in the paper's suburban office in the San Fernando Valley. My grandfather, Jack Carberry, was a sports columnist for the *Denver Post*. He was a character right out of the "Front Page" era of the business. He retired in 1961 as sports editor of *The Post* and died a year later on Thanksgiving Day in his apartment in Denver as he watched the Green Bay Packers play the Detroit Lions on television. I had met him only once, on a family camping trip to Colorado the year before he died.

The wire room, with its clackity-clacking teletype machines owned by the AP, UPI, Reuters and business and financial wire services, was our office and it was a noisy place. The teletypes had bells that would ring if an important story broke. An "advisory" was five bells, an "urgent" was seven and a "bulletin" was nine. The word URGENT or BULLETIN was printed above the dateline of the story. When students were shot by National Guardsmen during a Vietnam War protest at Kent State University in 1970, the AP national wire rang at least nine bells with the bulletin. There was another alert called SNAP, which rang more bells than a bulletin. The only "snap" anyone had seen before was when President Dwight D. Eisenhower died in 1965.

The editor of the day edition was Chuck Mosey. The *Times* called it the Preview, and later the Late Final, but around the newsroom it was known as The Mosey. It was sold only in street honor racks and at newsstands because it competed against the *Herald-Examiner*'s afternoon edition and also the evening news on TV.

The Late Final often contained weird and offbeat stories that Mosey cherished. Once, hundreds of squid washed up on several of L.A.'s beaches, reportedly because of warm currents that carried them farther north than usual.

Some of the squid were as long as four feet and, with their tentacles and sharp beaks, looked like creatures out of a science-fiction tale. Mosey played their arrival big on Page One, and his headline in large, bold type screamed, GIANT SQUID.

Mosey was known as Large Charles because he had a roly-poly physique and was at least 80 pounds overweight. He would occasionally stroll into the wireroom and read the stories on the teletypes. Once as his deadline neared, he came in and noticed that the stories on the Associated Press' main wire hadn't been trimmed. A long sheet of wire paper was on the floor and the copyboy who was supposed to cut and pass out the stories had disappeared. Mosey slowly rolled the string of stories up, reading them as he rolled. Suddenly he yelled, "Oh, shit!" On the floor was a bulletin that North Vietnamese president Ho Chi Minh had died. Large Charles wanted to blow a large gasket, but he didn't have time. The Preview was going to press in 15 minutes and he had to tear up the front page, put in Ho's death as the lead story and write a new banner headline that was in about 96-point type. It turned out the copyboy, Alex Purtee, had taken a lunch break. When Mosey had gotten the edition finished, he found Purtee and made it clear that he was never to leave the wireroom on a deadline.

There were ten copyboys and one copygirl, although, in the late 1960s, the paper began to expand its editorial staff, hiring men and women at a fairly even rate. As more women were added, the job title was changed from "copy boys" to "copy messengers."

Our boss was an Englishman named Terry Jacobson, who had worked at UPI as an entertainment reporter. He was also a musician and a chain smoker (cigarettes were permitted in the newsroom). He claimed that he wrote a song that Elvis Presley recorded, titled "Memories," but was never paid any royalties. Jacobson set up a bar in the wireroom's storage closet that was hidden behind the stacked rolls of teletype machine paper. If you needed to put a new roll of paper in the AP national wire machine, you had to move a bottle of bourbon to get the roll. A few of the editors knew about the bar and on occasion one would slip inside the closet for a quick pick-me-up after deadline. One afternoon, a copyboy named Steve Seiler dropped a bottle of good scotch on the floor. The room smelled heavenly but the Cutty Sark took the finish off the linoleum.

Jacobson fired Seiler, saying he couldn't come back until he replaced the scotch.

Drinking and, as its result, alcoholism were prevalent in the newsroom. Employees were encouraged to drink, and even pressured to join their bosses and colleagues after work, and sometimes even during their shift, at the Redwood House, the local saloon at the corner of Broadway and 1st Street in downtown Los Angeles. A female reporter, who had just started at the paper and felt uncomfortable about going alone into a bar, asked one of the older reporters to go with her and he said, "Why don't you just drink at your desk. Fewer people will see you."

Every afternoon at 4:30, one of the copy messengers would take a company car and drive to the bus station at Sixth and Main streets to pick up the Shipping Tables, a list of boat and ship arrivals and departures in L.A. harbor, which was printed daily in the financial section. The list would arrive on a Rapid Transit District bus from the Port of San Pedro and if it wasn't in the office by 6 p.m., the makeup editor would panic. Sometimes the copy messenger might stop to buy a hamburger or go home for the day with the list in his pocket.

Once I rode with a copyboy named Rick Hauser to the *Herald Examiner* to pick up a bundle of their latest edition for the *Times'* editors to peruse.

Usually, someone from the *Herald* would drop the stack off at the *Times'* guard station, but on this day, the papers never arrived. Workers at the *Her-Ex*, as we called it, were on strike and pickets were at the entrances, especially at the front door.

Arrangements had been made for us to park our car near the loading dock at the back of the building, go inside the Moorish-architecture landmark (a number of movies including some scenes from Jack Webb's newspaper film *30* had been shot there), and get the papers.

The guard gave us directions but we lost our way inside. Finally, we found the papers, but another guard wouldn't let us go out the way we had come in. He said we had to leave by the front exit where it was a chaotic scene. People who didn't honor the strike were crossing the picket line and the strikers yelled obscenities and threats at them. One picketer had a 35-millimeter camera and he took pictures of those who crossed the line. Hauser and I came out the front door and we hurried down the steps to the sidewalk. The person with the camera took our picture. We ran, scared, around the corner and back to the car.

Back at the *Times*, the night city editor wasn't very sympathetic when we told him what had happened. I was more worried that we had crossed the picket line because I had grown up in a Democratic Party home, and my mother said it was practically a mortal sin not to honor a picket line. It would put an indelible stain on my soul. As for getting our pictures taken, Hauser thought it was a bluff because the striker was taking so many pictures the camera had to be out of film.

We forgot about the *Herald* trip and went back to our job, which was fun most of the time. I was paid $85 a week, the most money I had ever made.

Before that, I cut lawns for $1.50 an hour and drove a delivery car for a chicken-and-fish restaurant called the Rowboat Cottage on Ventura Boulevard in the San Fernando Valley suburb of Sherman Oaks.

Although copy messengers performed menial tasks such as sharpen pencils, fill glue pots, chase down clips and photos from the paper's morgue and deliver mail and the latest editions of the paper to *Times* reporters in bureaus around the L.A. Civic Center, the job was a rally point to the coveted positions of reporter, copy editor, page layout editor and news editor.

If a copy messenger had ambition and showed potential to be a reporter, the first stop was the night weather desk where reports and forecasts from the U.S. Weather Bureau—which later became the National Weather Service—were edited.

The weather desk editor also had to answer the public information phone or, as the editors called it, the "nut phone." The elderly mother of the late actor Peter Lawford was a weekly caller. She had backed her Jaguar out of her driveway in Hollywood a little too fast and another car crashed into it. Her son had taken away her car keys. "Isn't there somebody there at the *Times* who can get them back for me?"

There were the usual calls from readers who had complaints that ranged from "Your reporters are communists" and "The Chandlers (the family who owned the *Times*) are left wingers," to "The type in your paper is too small, I can't read it." And, "The ink comes off on my hands. That doesn't happen when I read the *Wall Street Journal.*" Or, "I can't find the crossword puzzle." The accusations that the Chandlers were liberals and the reporters were communists were amusing because the *Times* had been a staunch Republican newspaper for decades and the Chandlers, with the exception of publisher Otis Chandler who steered the paper in a more mainstream direction, were a conservative dynasty that had ties to the John Birch Society. The rule was to listen for a couple of minutes, then politely hang up. Sometimes the caller wanted to settle a bet with a friend, or was lonely and just wanted another person to talk to.

There were bomb threats, too, which were taken seriously. When one would come in, the switchboard operators would immediately call the Los Angeles Police Department. Most of the threats were hoaxes except once when the cops did find a pipe bomb in a planter of ferns at the building's main entrance. Fortunately, it was a Saturday and that entrance was closed. The bomb didn't go off because the timer had malfunctioned, but the ferns were removed and the planter was filled in the next week.

The first responsibility of the weather desk editor, though, was to get the latest weather report in the paper. Rain was always news in Los Angeles. The night city editor was a crusty and cantankerous man named Glen Binford, and he was a stickler for accuracy, especially on weather forecasts. He sat at the city desk with his glasses perched on the bridge of his nose and a cigarette dangling from his mouth. He referred to the copy messengers as "young animals." The newsroom had an intercom system that worked when an editor on any desk pushed a button and a light would flash and a bell would ring on a panel in the wireroom. The panel had lights for the city desk, national desk, business and foreign. When the bell rang and the light came on for, say, the national desk, a copy messenger would push a button that turned off the light, then would see what the editor on the national desk wanted.

11

Binford had a small television on his desk and when the 11 p.m. news came on he would say to the weather desk editor, "Poke the prod and summon a young animal." He wanted to see the latest weather bureau forecast and compare it to the TV news' report. Usually they were the same, but when he left the office each night, Binford would stick his head in the wireroom to check the last forecast report.

If Binford liked you, he would refer to you by your last name. But if he didn't, or if he thought a person was incompetent, he would give them a nickname. He called one of the copyboys "Whip dick." A reporter whom he didn't like was the "OLP" (oily little prick). Another was "Satchel Ass." He called the religion writer "God" and the assistant religion writer "son of God." The state editor, who was Jewish, was "the Rabbi" and another editor with Middle Eastern heritage was the "Lebanese Leech" or "Bandit." Some nicknames weren't so offensive, like "bulldog" or "big dumb Swede kid," but once Binford branded a person, it was for life because soon the whole newsroom would know it.

One day, Jacobson announced that some of the copy messengers would get reporter training in the pressroom at Parker Center, the headquarters for the Los Angeles Police Department. It was July of 1969 and I was among five people whom Jacobson chose, with recommendations from the editors on the city desk, including Binford.

My shift in the pressroom, or "the police beat" as it was called, was from 7 a.m. to 3 p.m. on Saturdays and Sundays. It was good experience because it offered the chance to work on breaking news stories that involved the police and fire departments, and it also helped to develop a writing style that was clear and concise.

I parked my car, a Triumph TR4-A, on First Street in front of our offices and walked to Parker Center, a green eleven-story glass-and-steel building on Los Angeles Street, which was two blocks east of the *Times* building. I had to pin my press ID badge to my shirt so that the officers at the front desk would know who I was.

12

The pressroom was on the first floor and it had three desks, one for the *Times*, another for the *Herald-Examiner* and a third for City News Service, a local wire service. The reporters for the *Herald* and City News were Jeff Blake and Norman "Jake" Jacoby. Another newsman, named Bobby Voight, would sometimes fill in for Jacoby. All were veteran "cop shop" reporters and they, along with some in LAPD, resented that the *Times* used the pressroom as a training classroom. There was more than one instance when the *Herald*'s overnight reporter was suspected of purposely altering the facts in a story on his log, knowing in the morning that the *Times*' inexperienced copy messenger would read it, then phone it in to the city desk without first checking the story's facts, or lack of.

But, overall, I got along with the other reporters in the pressroom, and we needed each other's cooperation because several major stories broke on my weekends there. Among the biggest were the murders of Sharon Tate and four others by cult leader Charles Manson and his "family" of followers; the Chicano riots in East Los Angeles, in which respected Latino reporter Ruben Salazar was killed by a deputy sheriff's teargas canister as he ate lunch in a Whittier Boulevard restaurant called the Silver Dollar Cafe; and a deadly fire at a derelict downtown hotel named Ponet Square, in which twenty-two people died.

The call on the Manson murders came from the day watch commander at LAPD's West Los Angeles Division office. "Are you guys interested in five dead bodies?" asked the watch commander. Jeff Blake answered the cop's question with a question, "Are they in Watts?" "No," said the police officer. "Bel-Air." If the bodies had been in L.A.'s African-American neighborhood of Watts, where riots had taken place four years earlier, chances were the city desk would have wanted enough information to write a three- or four-paragraph story. Crime in the city's poorer neighborhoods was virtually ignored then by the media. Dorothy Chandler, the matriarch of the Chandler family, once sent a directive to the city desk. "No blood for breakfast," it said, which meant no car crashes, gory pictures or murders on Page 1. But five dead bodies in one of the wealthiest areas of the city, and one of the victims being the pregnant wife of director Roman Polanski, yes, we were very interested.

In the first half of the twentieth century, police reporters would go out and cover the fires, shootings and robberies, but the job had evolved into gathering information over the telephone in the pressroom, then entering the story in a log before phoning it to a reporter at the paper.

In my spare time at the police beat, I learned how to play poker from Voight and Blake, who were also veteran card players. We would bet quarters, and at first, I feared that gambling inside a police station would get me arrested, but I breathed easier when a detective from robbery homicide and a desk sergeant named Bill Keifer would join us. Keifer would come into the pressroom, walk over to a small refrigerator and put a brown paper bag that contained a pint of gin on the bottom shelf. The other cop usually dropped in about mid-afternoon. He had an ivory-handled revolver that he kept snug in a hip holster. He was a horse player, too, and he regularly took bets for Blake and Voight out to Santa Anita racetrack.

My weekends at Parker Center ended after two years, and I went back to the wireroom with its noisy, clackity teletypes in the late spring of 1971, to work nights as a copy messenger. Jacobson announced that some of us would get intern reporter jobs in the city room that summer. This was good news, but there was a catch. Once a copy messenger accepted an internship, there was no going back to the wireroom when it ended because another person would have filled your position. Either the *Times* hired you as a full-time reporter or you were out on the street to look for another job.

I was offered an internship but I was also enrolled in Cal State Los Angeles, where I was a political science major. Dial Torgerson, one of the best rewrite newspapermen around, urged me to take the internship. "You can go to school anytime," he said. But I also overheard Binford say that I wouldn't be hired when the internship was over because "Scheibe needs more police beating." I was stuck. I needed the job to pay for my apartment's rent and tuition. So, I played it safe and told Jacobsen I wanted to stay in the wireroom and do the intern job later. After a few weeks I realized I should have taken Torgerson's advice. While I was passing out papers and filling glue pots, my former mates were writing stories, many with bylines.

I avoided the city room and instead stayed in the wireroom to study, or would walk across the hallway to the sports department on my break and watch whatever game was on its black-and-white television set.

I knew a few people in sports, including Jack Simpson, the day desk assistant, Doug Smith, who was the son of columnist Jack Smith, and Ron Malloy, who also attended Cal State L.A. I also knew Chuck Garrity, the assistant sports editor, because he had worked for my grandfather at the *Denver Post* in the 1950s.

One afternoon, I was trimming stories from the Associated Press' state wire and Bill Shirley, the sports editor, came in and asked me if I would be interested in working as a night desk assistant in sports. He said Doug Smith had taken a reporter's job at one of the paper's suburban offices, and he needed to fill the position as soon as possible. Without hesitation I said, "Yes." Shirley shook my hand and said he'd see me in a week.

Word of my transfer to sports spread throughout the newsroom. "So, you're going to the Toy Department!" Binford said. "I hear you're going to be a jock sniffer," smirked Dave Larsen, a general assignment reporter.

Most of the comments were good-natured but there were hints of jealousy from some of the copy messengers and even from two of the reporters, who on one hand saw the sports section as a journalistic playground rather than a serious news gathering entity yet envied the freedom and creativity that sportswriters had, especially its feature writers. Sports had a culture that was different from the other sections at the paper. It had its own look, and when the design gurus tried to rein in sports makeup editors so that their pages would look like the rest of the paper's, they politely said "OK, we'll do that," then went back to what they had done before.

The sports department at night was borderline bedlam. Sometimes you couldn't hear the wire machines over the nightly din. The television was always on. People shouted at each other. A cloud of cigarette smoke floated near the ceiling until smoking was banned throughout the newsroom for fire safety and health reasons. The only exception was political cartoonist Paul Conrad, who was allowed to smoke a pipe at his drafting table.

Sports had its own dress code. While most people wore business attire (dress shirts, ties, jackets, and suits), the sports staff dressed like it had just walked in from a golf course pro shop. One night, Ted Green came to work in tennis shorts. He was scheduled as the rewrite person, but when Garrity saw Green's shorts, he ordered him to go home and put on long pants, explaining that tennis shorts crossed the line to inappropriate wear in a business office.

Green had just driven 20 miles in rush-hour traffic and didn't want to do it again. So he went to the pressroom and borrowed a pair of pants from one of the pressmen. They were dirty and streaked with black ink. But he put them on and returned to work his shift.

Between editions, a small football or a tennis ball would appear and there would be a game of four-corner catch. One night the football sailed over the partitions that separated sports from the rest of the newsroom and it landed on the desk of Al Bluhm, the executive news editor. Bluhm walked back, holding the ball, and said in a voice that crackled with doom, "I suggest you put this away."

Few positions came open in sports. Jack Simpson was only half-kidding when he said "the average guy on the street would give his right arm to come up here and answer the phones." But later, in the mid-1970s, Shirley was given the go-ahead by management to expand the staff, and he took his time, carefully selecting candidates from newspapers all over the United States. He said he wanted the *Times'* sports section to rival *Sports Illustrated* in its writing and photography.

16

Shirley was a former minor league pitcher from Arkansas. He worked at papers in San Diego, then came to the *Times* as an innovative makeup man. He rose to the position of executive sports editor, and became head of the department in 1968 when long-time sports editor Paul Zimmerman retired.

In the fall of 1971, the writing staff included Ross Newhan, John Weibush, Jeff Prugh, Dwight Chapin, Bob Oates, Shav Glick, Mal Florence, Lupi Saldana, Dan Hafner, and columnists Charles Maher, John Hall and Jim Murray. By 1979, Shirley had added Ron Rapoport, Skip Bayless, Ted Green, Scott Ostler, Don Merry, Mike Littwin, Richard Hoffer, Mark Heisler, Alan Greenberg, Cheryl Bentsen, Elizabeth Wheeler and Sheila Moran—an all-star lineup of sports journalists.

The copy desk was run by Garrity and it was considered the backbone of the department, although the writers didn't like to hear that. It flustered their egos. The copy editors wrote the headlines, edited the stories, cropped the photos and then wrote the captions for the photos. They read page proof galleys and, most of the time, caught the mistakes made by the writers and sometimes those edited into stories by other copy editors.

One afternoon, Garrity shouted, "You guys aren't reading the paper close enough. Too many mistakes are getting in."

Shirley always scheduled a writer to work a desk shift in case a story broke and a rewrite person was needed. At first, the writers grumbled about having to work a "desk trick," but most enjoyed the experience, and some even contributed a good headline. Mal Florence won an award when the Angels, a team that had been in existence for only a year, moved into first place on the Fourth of July in 1962. Before the American and National leagues were split into divisions, if a team was in first place on Independence Day it was given a good chance to win the pennant. Florence's headline read, "Heaven Can Wait, Angels in 1st on 4th."

Garrity was assisted by Jim Coontz, an easygoing, slow-talking makeup editor from Lubbock, Texas. Coontz was a page designer.

Garrity's copy editors were Frank Finch, Charlie Park, Harley Tinkham, Pat Ray, Jamie Curran, Avrum Dansky, Cal Whorton and Simpson. Later, Shirley would include George Kiseda, Robert Lochner, Jim Rhode, Larry Stewart, Mark McDonald, Dave Scheiderer, Tom Lamarre, Terry Shepherd and John Cherwa.

Finch, Park, and Whorton were the elders of the copy desk. Cal had been a PT boat commander during World War II. He first served in the Atlantic theatre, then he and his boat were transferred to the war in the South Pacific. Gen. Douglas MacArthur rode aboard Cal's boat into Manila Harbor in the Philippines.

Whorton was in the press box at the Coliseum in August of 1960 for a Rams exhibition game when Sen. John F. Kennedy of Massachusetts was brought in to meet the reporters and to watch the game. Kennedy was in Los Angeles to accept the Democratic Party's nomination for president at its convention, which was held at the Sports Arena next door. As Kennedy was led through the press box, he was introduced to L.D. Hotchkiss, who had been the editor of the *Times* in the 1950s. Hotchkiss was a conservative Republican and he refused to stand and shake Kennedy's hand. It obviously was an awkward moment for Kennedy who stood with his hand extended for a few moments until he silently pulled it away.

But Cal jumped out of his chair toward the senator and extended his hand.

"Jack, Cal Whorton, PT Boat Squadron, Philippine Islands." A look of relief came across Kennedy's face and the former commander of PT 109 gladly shook Cal's hand, and both talked for a few minutes about their time in the South Pacific.

The editors on the copy desk would kid Whorton about the incident, saying, "Hey Cal, you were skipper of a PT boat, how come you didn't get elected president?" Whorton usually ignored the ribbing, except for one time when he answered, "I don't know, but at least I didn't get my boat cut in half," referring to Kennedy's tragic incident that turned heroic in the Solomon Islands.

18

Finch and Park were both former baseball writers and Finch had covered pro football (the Rams, and the Dons of the old All-American Football Conference) and also boxing. In fact, before the Dodgers moved from Brooklyn in 1958, the Rams beat was the most coveted sports assignment in L.A., more than USC football, and the Rams were all Finch's.

Frank contracted polio when he was a boy and he wore a brace on his right leg that was attached to a special shoe. He walked with a noticeable limp, but it didn't slow him down. He was an avid reader and he had a fertile mind. He often stopped at the public library on his way to work to check out a book he had reserved, then would have it read by the time his shift had ended the same night.

The Rams of the early 1950s were a colorful team. They had won the 1951 NFL championship against the Cleveland Browns at the Coliseum, the only time an L.A. pro football team had ever won a title at home. Finch gave the Ram players appropriate nicknames. Elroy Hirsh was already known as "Crazylegs," a nickname that was bestowed on him at the University of Wisconsin because of the wild way his legs would propel him down the field. And quarterback Norm Van Brocklin was "the Dutchman." So Finch continued with the monikers. He named All-Pro defensive back Dick Lane "Night Train," because Lane loved to play, over and over again, the Buddy Morrow song of the same title. And Frank called Deacon Dan Towler, Dick Hoerner and Tank Younger—a trio of bulky running backs—the "Bull Elephant" backfield.

When it became more than a rumor that the Dodgers would move to Los Angeles, Finch asked to be taken off the Rams and put on one of the town's two Pacific Coast League teams—the Angels and Hollywood Stars—so that he could learn how to cover baseball. Although some members of the *Times* editorial board were against the Dodgers' move to the West Coast (there was a sign in the newsroom that said, "Keep the Dodgers out of L.A."), Finch wrote positive and promotional stories about how beneficial it

19

would be for the city to have a major league baseball team. It would give L.A. the big-league status that even the Rams hadn't provided. Finch's articles helped sway public and political opinion in favor of Walter O'Malley's plan, and when the Dodgers arrived, sports editor Paul Zimmerman awarded the beat to Finch.

Frank was a florid writer, although some of the descriptive phrases would be inappropriate today because they were either too clicheish or ethnically insensitive. His stories were sprinkled with such lines as "round-tripper" for a home run and a "four-ply swat" for a grand-slam. A double was "a two-bagger," an easy fly ball "a can of corn" or "a can of succotash." When the bases were loaded, "the sacks were saturated," and a "Texas Leaguer" was a bloop hit to the outfield. On a story about Minnesota Twins pitcher Morris Titanic being sent to the minors, the headline Finch wrote said, "Titanic Goes Down."

But the term "Chinese Home Run," a round-tripper that would take the shortest route out of the ballpark, would regularly appear in game stories.

Finch once described a Frank Howard fly ball that barely dropped over the left-field screen in the Coliseum as a home run that came down "dripping with egg fu-yung." He covered the team until his brace-saddled leg would no longer allow him to climb the stairs at some of the older National League ballparks.

Whether he was covering the Dodgers or working a shift on the copy desk, Finch's wit was ever-present. Once he was walking down Second Street on his way to the office. He passed a row of pressmen sitting on the sidewalk near a side entrance to the *Times*. Several of them, their clothes and hands stained black, were reading copies of the edition they had just printed. It was in the 1950s and Otis Chandler was being groomed by his father, Norman Chandler, to succeed him as publisher of the paper. The elder Chandler and his wife, Dorothy, wanted their son to become familiar with every department of the *Times*, and this learning process included a stint in the pressroom. He sat dressed in navy blue pants and shirt with his name written on a patch over his shirt pocket. He stood out among the other workers, the blond surfer and ex-shotputter from Stanford who was about to take the reins of the family business. Finch saw Otis, limped up to him and bent down, saying, "I've got my eye on you. You're going places."

Charlie Park was slight in stature, with wispy, sandy hair, and he had crinkly face with glasses. He had covered the Dodgers for the *L.A. Mirror News*, an afternoon newspaper that was owned by the Chandlers. During the baseball season, beat writers could earn extra money, as much as $50 a game, by working as official scorekeepers. Park kept score on the night of June 30, 1959, when pitcher Sam Jones of the San Francisco Giants had a no-hitter going against the Dodgers at the Coliseum. In the eighth inning with two out, Jim Gilliam hit a grounder that bounced over the mound. Shortstop Andre Rodgers charged the ball, gloved it and then dropped it trying to get the speedy Dodger second baseman at first.

Everyone held their breath as Park turned to Finch, who was sitting next to him, and asked, "What do you think?" Frank said, "I think it's a hit." Park agreed and ruled it an infield single. His decision brought a swift negative reaction from many in the crowd, the San Francisco writers and the Giants players.

"If I fielded the ball cleanly, I would have thrown him out," Rodgers said afterward. Jones finished with a one-hitter and a 2-0 shutout. "Imagine anyone calling that a hit," he said with tears in his eyes. "I guess they just don't want no-hitters thrown here."

Park tried to convince Jones that Gilliam would have beaten the throw, but Sam, like everyone else in the Giants clubhouse, wasn't buying Charlie's reasoning. Park was criticized by the San Francisco media and instead of shaking it off, he took it personally and, for years, was reluctant to talk about the call.

Harley Tinkham was a world-class expert on track and field. He graduated from Hollywood High School then went to USC and lettered in the high jump and decathlon for the Trojans' 1943 national championship team. When he worked for the *Mirror* in the early 1950s, Tinkham would leave the paper on Friday nights in the spring, get on a Greyhound bus bound for Bakersfield and compete the next day in all-comers meets that drew the best athletes from up and down the state. One of Tinkham's competitors in the decathlon was Olympic champion Bob Mathias.

Harley was known as "The Ace" because that's what he called people whom he liked. It was a compliment if he said, "Hey, Ace, could you look something up for me?" In turn, all his colleagues called him Ace. He had a mane of silver wavy hair and he wore dark glasses when he worked the copy desk.

His eccentricity extended to his Christmas shopping, which he always did for his family late at night on Christmas Eve at a local drugstore chain.

Pat Ray was a grumpy former race car driver who complained a lot, but he had a heart of gold. "Why are we running this piece of crap," he would say when Garrity gave him a story to edit. Chuck usually ignored him and put up with his whining because Pat was a good editor, knew auto racing and golf inside and out, and worked fast on a deadline. He toiled in the pits at the Indianapolis 500 and drove sprint cars competitively as a hobby before he became an auto racing writer in the 1950s. He also had been an officer in U.S. Army Intelligence during the Korean War. His father, Bob Ray, was a baseball writer who covered teams in the Pacific Coast League. Pat was born near 41st Street and Avalon, the intersection where L.A.'s old Wrigley Field once stood.

He liked to tell stories about his auto racing days, especially the yarn when he and his pit crew were trying to get some sleep in the basement of a house the night before the Indy 500. Fans were partying all over Indianapolis and one reveler who had drank too much beer decided to urinate through a ground-level window of the house, and onto Ray and the crew.

Jamie Curran was a makeup editor from Nebraska who had a facial resemblance to comedian Stan Laurel. He played tennis on the Cornhuskers men's varsity, but his passion was college football. He wrote a column in the Saturday paper that analyzed the best games scheduled for that weekend. Curran was a quiet sort, but he had a temper. If the Nebraska football team won, Jamie would come to work as happy as a lark. But if the Huskers lost, all of us let him suffer in silence. Once when Oklahoma beat Nebraska, Curran came to work and found Ted Green casually sitting in his chair, with his feet up on Curran's desk. Jamie snapped, "Do you want to make up this section?" Green quickly got up and left.

Dan Hafner probably covered more of L.A.'s teams than any sportswriter before or after him. From the early 1960s through the mid-1970s, Hafner could be found in the press box at an Angels, Dodgers, Lakers and Kings game, plus at ringside for championship fights from the Forum and Olympic Auditorium to Las Vegas. Hafner was from Hannibal, Missouri, and his grandfather ran a ferry that carried passengers across the Mississippi River to Illinois. When Danny went home to Hannibal for vacation, the town would celebrate by hosting the Dan Hafner Invitational golf tournament, which was played on a 9-hole course. On the desk, Hafner wrote the baseball, NBA and NHL roundups.

Avrum Dansky kept track of the agate page, where readers could find box scores, golf and tennis results, cross-country times, even catches by anglers at local saltwater sportfishing docks. It was called agate because that was the size of the type, about 6 point, although there was a smaller size at 5.5 called Ruby.

Dansky also oversaw the high school sports staff, and ruled like a tyrant over a group of young part-timers who took the scores and summaries of games from high-school age stringers. One night, Dansky tore into a kid who had made an error on a basketball box score—the players' point totals didn't add up to the final score. The kid was so flustered he lit two cigarettes at the same time. A prep kid once challenged Dansky to a fight in a parking lot across the street from the paper after Avrum had berated him over typing a wrong score.

Dansky just wanted the stats to be correct. He kept up-to-date records of every player in major league baseball. The NBA, too. His books were so accurate the baseball writers would often come

23

into the office after a game or a trip to check their stats with his, or look up numbers on a player that they were writing a feature story on.

Avrum had played basketball at Marshall High School in Los Angeles, then graduated from UCLA. He was the fastest typist anyone had ever seen and he could quickly add columns of numbers in his head. His only vice was gambling. He didn't smoke, didn't drink, didn't spend money on cars and clothes.

He wasn't married, so he had no responsibilities for wife and family. But he loved the racetrack and the poker clubs in Gardena.

On an occasional Friday night after work, he would catch the last flight to Las Vegas from the Burbank airport and then would play blackjack all night, usually at the MGM Grand Hotel. When it got light, he would fly back in time for work the next day.

We always knew if Avrum had won or lost. If he was smiling, Avrum had won big, but if he was sullen, it had been a bad night at the tables. Dansky wasn't a high roller, but he could have been if he wasn't so devoted to the newspaper business. He had so much money he would leave uncashed paychecks in his desk drawer, an oversight that would prompt the *Times'* payroll department to plead with him to go the bank because he was backing up their books.

One night at the blackjack table, he was informed by the casino's manager that the tabs for his room and dinner would be paid by the hotel. As he continued to play, two "hostesses" approached him and in a soft voice one of them asked, "Mr. Dansky, if you would like anything, anything at all," to let them know. Avrum looked up at the two women. "There is something you can do for me." One woman leaned closer and asked in a whisper what it was. Dansky asked, "Can you get me a ride to the airport?"

Avrum loved oldies rock 'n' roll, especially songs by Elvis Presley and the Beach Boys, and on Presley's birthday he would wear a black T-shirt with red letters on the front that said "The King."

These were the people I would work with. On my first night in sports, Garrity said, "Welcome to the bigs, kid"

At first, it was a struggle. I accidentally sent the photographs for the front page through the pneumatic tube system to the composing room instead of first taking them to the art department where they would be airbrushed by the paper's artists. The edition was late because of my error. Garrity's face was beet red and I stayed out of his way for a few days. Once, four reports from fish landings were phoned in at the same time and I asked Charlie Park if he could take a couple. He shot back at me, "I'm not the fish editor."

My shift was 3 p.m. to 11:30 p.m., five and sometimes six days a week. I answered the phones, trimmed the game and news stories from the sports wires, edited horse race charts, and wrote game highlights for ABA basketball and WHA hockey games. The Edmonton Oilers had a young teenager named Gretzky who seemed to make his team's scoring summary every game. The New Jersey Nets had a player from the University of Massachusetts who could jump from the free-throw line and dunk the basketball. His teammates called him Dr. J. I wrote feature stories on horse racing and soccer, on my own time, and during football season helped the writers by getting locker room quotes after USC and UCLA games. At 23, I was the youngest full-time member of the staff. And I loved every day there. Getting my degree quickly became an afterthought, something I foolishly convinced myself I would do later. During the day I'd play golf with Tinkham, Hafner and Florence. If there was an opening in the foursome, Garrity or Al Franken, a public relations czar in L.A. whose clients included the Sunkist Indoor track and field meet and an annual boat show, would fill in. In the afternoon, it was back to the sports department merry-go-round.

After deadline at 11:30, the desk crew went for a beer at the Redwood. If it was closed, then it was Anthony's, the pressmen's bar, or the Shortstop on Sunset Boulevard, which was once owned by Bob Hunter of the *Herald-Examiner*. The Shortstop was located just below Dodger Stadium and the majority of its patrons were off-duty LAPD cops, but a few Dodgers would regularly stop in after a game, including Steve Yeager, Reggie Smith and umpire Bruce Froemming. Fans and some baseball groupies frequented the bar when the Dodgers were home and Tom Lasorda eventually declared the Shortstop off-limits to his players.

But the Redwood was the liveliest place, attracting attorneys, newspaper people, detectives, boxing promoters (the Main Street Gym was two blocks away), and secretaries from around the civic center. During the Manson Family trial at the courthouse downtown, which was covered by a national corps of journalists, the Redwood was the hot bar in L.A.

After the Redwood closed for the evening, we would have breakfast at the Pantry, a popular restaurant on Figueroa Street that was open 24 hours. I'd get home about 5 a.m., get two or three hours sleep, then drive to Griffith Park or Rancho Park for golf.

The year 1972 was highlighted by the Olympic Games in Munich and the Lakers' glorious run to the NBA championship that included their 33-consecutive-game win streak. The Dodgers played in the World Series in 1974 against the Oakland A's, and again in 1977 and 1978 against the Yankees. USC won national championships in football and UCLA matched those with titles in basketball. Muhammad Ali fought Joe Frazier in Manila, and then George Foreman in Kinshasa, Zaire. Although these historic events made it exciting to work in sports, I had virtually no hand in covering them. For me, it was WHA highlights and horse race charts, mixed with the occasional feature, again written on my own time.

When Jeff Prugh suddenly quit the sports department to join the *Times'* national bureau in Atlanta, I applied for his job. Shirley accepted my résumé but I never got an interview. Instead, he told me I would have to be "more aggressive." "I can't send you out to Dodger Stadium," he said. Then a position was created for a full-time writer to cover high school sports. I applied again but Shirley had his eye on a writer from the *Pasadena Star News* named Chris Baker, who was African-American. There were no minorities in sports other than Lupi Saldaña, who covered fishing and outdoors.

Lupi had worked at the paper for years, and although he was Hispanic, he wasn't thought of as a minority. Lupi was Lupi.

"I hired a black man," Shirley proudly stated when I asked about the high school writing job. I was 0-for-2 and the average didn't improve as, one after another, writers from other papers joined the staff. A reporter on cityside named Bill Drummond said, "You can't start at the top. You're better off going some place else for five years, then come back."

Ted Beitchmann, who had worked in sports at the *Philadelphia Bulletin* before he came to the *Times* as features section editor, said, for him, "Sports was like quicksand. You get stuck on the desk and you can't get out." I told him I didn't mind getting stuck as long as I had a good job. He said if that's what I wanted, "it wasn't going to happen by osmosis." One girl I really liked said she was disappointed in me because "your job is a dead end...you're going nowhere."

I knew all of them were right, but my heart was in that sports department.

Though I didn't want to leave its Neverland world, I reluctantly decided to update my résumé and found the addresses of the suburban papers in the L.A. area, and the *Denver Post*, my grandfather's old paper. Then, a telephone call came to the copy desk on a Saturday night in late January of 1979, that would have a profound effect on the paper and, eventually, me. Something had happened to Jim Murray.

Chapter Two

I Don t Want to Bore You

"He that is strucken blind cannot forget the
precious treasure of his eyesight lost."
—William Shakespeare

The house was at the end of a cul-de-sac on a hill that overlooked Sunset Boulevard at the west end of Bel-Air. Peggy Lee lived in a tan two-story house on the corner. Across a canyon were nestled the homes of some of Hollywood's top producers, actors and studio executives. Rams owner Carroll Rosenbloom and his wife Georgia lived a few blocks away and Bel-Air Country Club was just down the hill.

The driveway led up to a beautiful home with a large garage. There were flower pots and azalea bushes near the front porch, which was made of brick. A hose trickled drops of water down the steps as if someone had just watered the plants.

It had been six months since Gerry Murray had made that call to the sports desk. She told Chuck Garrity that Jim wouldn't be able to write a column for the Super Bowl because he was in the hospital. He had undergone emergency eye surgery for a detached retina after his eye started to bleed while he was on a horse race outing with other sportswriters at Gulfstream Park in Miami. The retina, a thin layer of nerve tissue on the inside of the eyeball that transmits information from the eye to the brain, was reattached and it stayed up for a while, but then it came off again. Doctors at the Jules Styne Institute at UCLA and specialists at the General Hospital in Boston tried to restore the sight in Murray's left eye, but it never came back.

To make things worse, he had a cataract on his right eye that was maturing or, as his doctors called it, "ripening." They were hesitant to take it off because there was a good chance the retina on that eye would come off, too. Murray was told that retinas sometimes come loose after a fall or blow to the head. In December of 1978, he and Gerry had been in Hawaii for the World Cup of Golf at the Princeville courses on Kauai. Early one morning when it was still dark, the telephone rang in the condo where they were staying. Jim got up to answer it and, unfamiliar with the floor plan in the dark, tripped over a coffee table and fell, hitting his head on the way down.

Now the world looked to him like it was permanently eight o'clock at night.

People were shadowy outlines. Murray's first column since before the Super Bowl game appeared in the *Times* on July 1, 1979. He was the master of making sports a metaphor for life, adding the timing of a great comic, but he decided to leave the comedy out of that one. The headline said, "If you're expecting one-liners, wait a column." He wrote how "he had lost an old friend" and that he was now known as "ol' blue eye." He wanted to tell his readers why he had been away. "I feel I owe my friends an explanation as to where I've been all these weeks. Believe me, I would rather have been in a press box." It was an emotional article filled with memories of the things he had seen all the way back to his childhood. His secretary, Marilyn White, helped type it. Afterward, she came into the office in tears, saying to Bill Shirley that she couldn't go through it again.

So Shirley put out the word that someone from the staff would be assigned to work with Murray. The job involved driving him to events, doing research and interviews, reading to him and whatever else it took to get his column written.

The editors at the *Times* feared that if Murray's column was absent any longer, the paper would lose circulation. One noted that the sports section looked like it had a big hole in it each morning. Garrity said, "Whoever works with Murray is going to have a great job."

My search for a job at another paper was still in progress when Garrity recommended me to work with Murray. Chuck knew that I lived in Brentwood, just five minutes by car from Jim's house in Bel-Air.

Two days passed but Shirley hadn't made a decision. I found out later that he wasn't sure if I could do it. Shirley said to Garrity, "I don't know, Chuck, he's awful young." But Garrity wasn't worried. "Scheibe will come through. You can count on him." So, Shirley called me into his office and said the job with Murray was mine if I wanted it. That night Jim phoned me and he was concerned. "I don't want to bore you…I don't want you to be bored," he said.

Jim said he could get one of his three sons, Tony, Ted, or Rick, to drive him. "They can bring their guitars and wait for me." But he didn't sound too convinced that the idea would work. I assured him that I wouldn't get bored and that I wanted to work with him. It was an assignment and I was getting paid for it. Murray asked me if I could come over to his house the next day at 10 a.m., and I said yes. I hung up the phone, and wondered how anyone could be bored working with Jim Murray.

The next morning, I drove my red 1969 Mustang down the hill to the end of the cul-de-sac on Bellagio Terrace, then up a steep driveway that led to a pretty, split-level house with a bay window that had a sweeping view of Los Angeles. The west end of Bel-Air is not a neighborhood one would expect a newspaperman to live in.

31

But to afford a house on Bellagio Terrace, the Murrays had traded up twice in the lucrative L.A. real estate market, first with a modest home in the Pacific Palisades area of Los Angeles, followed by an expansive ranch house on an acre and a quarter of land that overlooked the Pacific Ocean in Malibu. He sold that house to pop music icon Bob Dylan.

Before he made a down payment on his Bel-Air home, Murray had bid on a house in the Palisades. This one overlooked the 18th fairway at the Riviera Country Club. He said he always dreamed that one day he'd own a house where he could step out the back door and tee up a golf ball. The dream that he'd own a home on his favorite golf course, called "Hogan's Alley" after his hero, Ben Hogan, was too good to come true. Murray was outbid and he settled for a house a few miles east.

"You can't go wrong with California real estate," Jim once said. "I couldn't have bought this house on a journalist's salary."

I parked my car and walked up to the front door. I was nervous and tried to clear my throat and swallow, but it was dry. I knocked on the door waited, clasping my hands together, rubbing my sweaty palms on my hip pockets. I heard footsteps and the door opened. Jim Murray stood there, dressed in a long-sleeve white shirt and dark trousers, his black, curly hair combed back. He looked at me through his thick glasses. The left lens was thicker than the right one and it magnified the grotesqueness of his dead eye. I tried not to look at it as he tried to see who I was.

Before he lost his eyesight, Murray would come into the sports department on Friday afternoon to deliver his Sunday column to Jim Coontz, who made up an early edition of the Sunday paper called the bulldog. The bulldog was filled with feature stories that would be subbed out on Saturday with game stories and news updates. Murray walked past the copy desk, handed Coontz his column, which was typed on light brown drawing paper. Then he would walk over to Marilyn White's desk to get his mail, stick his head inside Shirley's office to say hello, and leave as quietly as he came in.

The younger writers and editors would stare at him in awe. One night, there was a question about a fact in Murray's column. The editor was too afraid to call Jim at home. Garrity said, "Come on, Murray's a good guy." Dan Hafner was a copy boy at the *L.A. Examiner* in the 1940s when Murray worked there after he had moved to Los Angeles from Hartford, Connecticut. "Even then as a young reporter in nineteen forty-four," Hafner said, "you could see that Murray was special."

I felt like that copy editor who was afraid to call him. I stammered, "Hi, Jim, I'm John Scheibe." He said, "Yes, I remember you. Come in."

I followed him through the foyer and into a spacious family room. On one wall hung thirteen gold plaques, each an award for national sportswriter of the year.

On the opposite wall over a fireplace was a large painting of a young Murray sitting behind a manual typewriter at an old wooden desk. The artwork was done by Gene Wiley who had played center for the Lakers in the early 1960s. Murray offered me a seat on a long couch near the awards wall. Two bowls of baseballs sat on a large bar at one end of the room. At the other end was a picture window that had a panoramic view of the city.

He asked me what sports l liked. I told him I liked the major ones, especially golf and baseball. He asked me what teams I liked and I said the L.A. teams, the Dodgers. He said he liked the Dodgers too. I told him that my grandfather was once the sports editor of the *Denver Post*. Murray said he knew of Jack Carberry because he had been a stringer for *Sports Illustrated* when Murray helped start up the magazine in 1954. Jim said one of the first things that he did in the morning before he lost his eyesight was to read the box scores, to see how players such as Pete Rose, Reggie Jackson, Joe Morgan and Steve Garvey had done in their games the night before.

He said his two biggest problems were that he couldn't look up facts and statistics and he couldn't drive a car. He added, "I can call up Jim Palmer on the phone anytime but it's not the same as interviewing someone in person." He said sometimes he could tell a lot about a person by just watching him or her. One player was former Dodgers shortstop Maury Wills. "With Wills, nothing was wasted, everything he did had a purpose," Murray said. "He'd come into the clubhouse, get dressed, open his mail, make sure his glove and bats were ready for the game, and then go out on the field."

So, I would be Murray's eyes, to look up stats, to read and drive, but also to be an observer. At first I didn't catch on that this was going to be the difficult part, to pick out what Jim would be interested in. My first test in observing would come one day at Dodger Stadium when he asked me to follow Davey Lopes before a game and to watch everything that the second baseman did.

After Jim explained what my duties would be, he said that Lynn Shackleford, the former All-American basketball star at UCLA who had become a local TV sports broadcaster, was on his way over to do an interview about Jim's return to writing. Could I come back the next day and drive him to the Forum in Inglewood for a luncheon with Muhammad Ali? I said yes, and that was the end of my visit. Gerry Murray came into the room and Jim introduced us. She was a very cheery and pleasant woman, and she had a great laugh.

I said goodbye and drove back home, but when I got there I was so excited I couldn't sit down. That night, I told Garrity that I was taking Murray to see Ali. He said, "Keep a journal, kid." It was good advice. I found a reporter's notebook in the office supply cabinet and it fit perfectly in my back pocket.

****

In the summer of 1979, the sports world watched Eammon Coghlan of Ireland beat America's best miler, Steve Scott, in Philadelphia, in a time of 3:52.9; John McEnroe overwhelm Tim Gullickson in straight sets at Wimbledon; and the U.S. men's basketball team deliver its gold-medal-winning performance at the Pan-Am Games in San Juan, Puerto Rico. Bob Knight, the coach of the U.S. team, had caused an international disturbance when he struck a San Juan police officer. Mal Florence was in San Juan to cover the games for the *Times* and remembered that Knight, whose contentious relationship with the media has been well documented, went out of his way to be gracious to the U.S. writers because, "for once he needed us," Florence said. Knight made it out of the country without being arrested but he was convicted in absentia and received a six-month sentence.

Boxing fans saw Muhammad Ali retire that same year at age 37. Ali later would unretire himself and fight Larry Holmes in 1980, but he used this first announcement to help promote a musical extravaganza that would benefit the U.S. Olympic boxing program.

Murray's and Ali's paths had crossed several times, first in July of 1962 at a press party in Beverly Hills before Ali, who was known then as Cassius Clay, fought Alejandro Lavarante of Argentina. Again in Lewiston, Maine, for his second fight against Sonny Liston. In Kinshasa, Zaire, when Ali fought George Foreman, and when Ali met Holmes in the parking lot at Caesar's Palace.

At the Beverly Hills press party, Gerry Murray, who loathed boxing, went up to Ali and Lavarante and said, "Why do you two beautiful men want to hurt each other?" Jim said you could see the light go on in Ali's head: "I'm so pretty!"

In October of 1974, Murray followed Ali and Foreman to the outposts of central Africa to cover their heavyweight championship fight. The "Rumble in the Jungle," as it was called, was scheduled to start about 7 p.m. Los Angeles time, four o'clock in the morning in Zaire. The *Times* had arranged to have an open phone line at ringside so that Murray and Dial Torgerson, who had become the paper's correspondent for that area of Africa, could file their stories directly to the copy desk.

The fight took place in a torrential rainstorm and by the time Ali knocked Foreman out in the eighth round, the water was up over the ankles of the writers at ringside. Murray began to dictate his column to Avrum Dansky, but about halfway through, his voice started to fade and grew fainter by the word until there was only static on the line. For an hour, Dansky called into the phone, "Helllooooo, Jim Murray…"

The *Times'* operators desperately tried to reconnect the line, and no one was more concerned than Chuck Garrity. It was the only time anyone had seen panic on his face. One of the biggest upsets in boxing history (Ali was a heavy underdog) and certainly one of the biggest sports events of the year and your number one writer's column was in danger of not getting into the paper.

In producing a daily sports section, there was a fine line between a good night and a bad one. All it took to have things go over a cliff was for a story to be late, a photographer to miss a deadline for a front-page picture or to be shorthanded of copy editors. With only half of Murray's column in hand and the other still in Zaire, the wheels were quickly coming off.

The first edition's deadline went by and there was no Murray column. The deadline for the night's second edition, the one delivered to subscribers' homes the next morning, was approaching. Suddenly, the phone on Dansky's desk rang. It was Murray. He had gone back to his hotel and got a clear line from his room. His column made some of the home delivery and it was reprinted in all of the editions the next day.

"Ali tumbled Foreman on his ear at 2:58 of the 8th round early today after beating him into a lump for the first seven rounds. Foreman went down like a guy falling out of a seven-story window. He tried to get up but he didn't know which way it was."

Now, on a cloudy morning nearly five years later, Murray and Ali would meet again. Jim walked up to a crowd of writers and television crews that had gathered outside the Forum's entrance at the corner of Manchester Boulevard and Prairie Avenue in Inglewood, the plot of land where Jack Kent Cooke had built his Roman-columned arena. The newsmen warily eyed Murray, unsure of what to say to him. Even *Times* columnist John Hall and sportscaster Stu Nahan, both of whom knew Jim well, shifted their weight from one foot to the other, a little shy to greet their colleague whom they hadn't seen in six months.

Then, a baby-blue Lincoln limousine pulled up. The door opened and out stepped Jerry Buss, the Lakers' new owner who had recently bought the NBA franchise and the L.A. Kings hockey team from Cooke. Jack needed the cash to pay for an expensive divorce settlement. Buss was a wealthy real estate developer and this luncheon was his "coming out" to the L.A. media.

He appeared nervous as he put on his jacket and looked around at the crowd. He saw Murray and a smile broke out on his face. "Hey, Jim, how are you?" They shook hands, and the greeting broke the ice with the rest, who closed around Murray, some calling out to him. With his press agent Bob Steiner leading the way, Buss took Murray by the arm and everyone followed. Murray turned to me and said that he was going to see Ali in a private room before the lunch started and he'd meet me later.

The luncheon tables were set up on the basketball floor and a buzz started around the arena when Buss and Murray walked in. Actor Ryan O'Neal, who was a fight manager himself, yelled, "Jim, Jim Murray." Murray, Buss and Steiner disappeared and I sat down at a table near the dais, where Ali would later take questions.

During the press conference, Ali said that he "was tired of beating people up for a living" and that his joining Islam was the most courageous gamble he had taken because "this country is owned and controlled by Jews." A newsman near the front challenged this remark and Ali explained, quite unconvincingly, that what he meant was that since he was so much loved in Arab countries, the friends of Israel were bound to misunderstand. Murray pointed out that Ali had "gotten away with such dangerous demagoguery and reckless rhetoric before because politicians and even the media would rather oppose motherhood than Muhammad."

Then, in typical Ali bombast, he closed the questioning with, "I played the fool but was the wise man in the end."

Afterward, I drove Murray back to his house and I could tell that he had enjoyed himself. It was the first time he'd covered an event since January and his lack of eyesight hadn't interfered. I read him the notes I had taken, and later he wrote: *"But the conquering Lion of Louisville, the desert shriek, the on-again, off-again boxing champion of the universe for lo! these many years, Muhammad Ali, went out the same way he came in—full of boasting, breast-beating, full of evangelical fervor one minute and hortatory soapboxing the next, as cockily abrasive at his exit as he was at his entrance 20 years ago.*

"No telltale scar tissue loomed above his eyes, his lips were neither swollen or stitched, he had all his teeth and both his ears and his voice was as loud and clear as a hog caller's. His face didn't even look as if it had spent the last 19 years in a chorus line, let along a ring. This was no broken-down pug trying to sort out scrambled images in the brain, this was a man whose tongue was as nimble as a carnival spieler's."

****

I was back at Murray's the next day at 10 a.m. We went to his office, which was down a steep, carpeted staircase off the family room, on the first level of the house. It was an airy room with a big window that faced west toward the ocean. In the summer afternoon, the breeze from Santa Monica Bay was a delight coming through the screen. In front of the window were his desk and a comfortable leather chair. A large walk-in closet had been converted into a library, its shelves filled with mostly sports books. Murray felt his way with his hands until he located a file cabinet and asked me to dig out a *Time* magazine cover story that he had written on Walter O'Malley. Jim said he went to the Dodgers' spring training camp at Vero Beach, Florida, and spent two weeks with O'Malley before the start of the 1958 season. Now, O'Malley had been diagnosed with cancer and Jim wanted to write a tribute column to the man who had helped expand baseball nationwide.

I found the article and Murray asked me to read it to him. It was a long story, about 10,000 words, and I quickly discovered that reading out loud wasn't easy. I stumbled over words and had to back up and repeat phrases and even sentences. Then my voice started to crack and I had to clear my throat several times. A glass of water didn't help. I struggled for about 30 minutes until Murray said he had heard as much as he needed for background information.

I put the story back in the file cabinet. Next to it was a pile of tote bags and briefcases that writers are given when they cover a major sports event, such as a Super Bowl or World Series. Murray told me to pick one out for myself, so I took the one on top, which was a zippered bag from an NFC championship football game.

It was getting close to noon and Jim suggested we go out to lunch. I drove the Mustang over to Love's Barbecue, a ribs restaurant that he liked on San Vicente Boulevard in Brentwood. It was quiet and cool inside, and after we had ordered, Jim talked about his days on the Hollywood beat for *Time* in the 1950s. He reached into his pocket and took out a solid gold money clip that Jack Benny had given him. The clip had Benny's famous deadpan caricature engraved on the front. On the back was a personal sentiment. The comedian had given it to Murray after Jim started to write for the *Times* in February of 1961. When he began, Jim found it difficult to compose a column six times a week. It was a tough assignment and he had trouble finding the column's voice and a direction to take it. But Benny told him to be himself, advice that was as golden as the money clip. He discovered his touch on a trip with the Dodgers. On an off day for the team in Cincinnati, Murray poked fun at the Ohio rivertown, with lines such as "They still haven't finished the freeway…it's Kentucky's turn to use the cement mixer." With that playful spirit, he was off and running.

Whatever event he covered, Jim tried to work in a zinger at the city he was in. On Minneapolis-St. Paul: "They didn't like each other and from what I could see, I didn't blame them either." St. Louis: "It had a bond issue recently and the local papers campaigned

for it on a slogan 'Progress or Decay,' and decay won in a landslide."
Spokane: "The only trouble with Spokane, Wash., as a city is that
there is nothing to do there after 10 o'clock. In the morning." San
Francisco: "It fancies itself Camelot, but comes off more like
Cleveland. Its legacy to the world is the quiche." New York: "In New
York, you look out the window of your hotel room and the view is a
brick wall."

Officials of the Indianapolis 500 were ready to run Murray out
of town when, after two deadly crashes that involved Eddie Sachs
and Dave MacDonald at the Speedway in the 1960s, he referred to
the race as the "run for the lilies," and in a column that parodied the
500, he began one sentence with "Gentlemen, start your coffins."

At the Kentucky Derby, he called the city of Louisville "the
nation's bar towel."

The only town he had anything good to say about was Montreal.
But the city he adored was Los Angeles. "I love every brick and
palm tree," he said at a dinner that honored him and then *Times* publisher Tom Johnson. "In L.A., there are Pacific sunsets, every Rose
Bowl game ever played and the earthquakes come with the geraniums." He was once asked in a magazine article what he liked most
about L.A. He said that he enjoyed looking up into the blue sky to
see a jet airplane fly over and feeling glad that he wasn't on it.

In 1960, Murray's boss at *Time* and *Life* said, "Jim, I've got
good news and bad news. The bad news is we want you to come
back [to New York] and work."

The oppressive humidity in the summer and the freezing temperatures in the winter were two of the reasons Murray left
Hartford 16 years earlier. There were no Pacific sunsets or seats
on the aisle at box office premieres or geraniums growing in
Times Square. Jim said, "If that's the bad news, I don't want to
hear the good news." Their good news was *Time* and *Life* wanted
him to be the managing editor of *Sports Illustrated*.

The *Time* and *Life* editor pleaded, "How can I get you back
here?" Jim said, "The only way you'll get me back there is in
chains." And he took *Times* managing editor Frank McCullough

and publisher Otis Chandler up on their offer to write a sports column for his adopted home town's top newspaper.

As our lunch was served, Jim said it would always amuse him when someone accused him of misquoting them, because he rarely quoted anyone. "A column has a beginning, a middle and an end. You say what you have to say, then get out," he said. In his contract, he and the *Times* agreed that the column would be played down the left-hand side of the front page of the sports section and that an etched caricature of Murray would appear near the top of the column.

Another celebrity Murray had contact often with was Bing Crosby. Jim would run into the singer at Del Mar and at Santa Anita, and also at Crosby's national pro-am golf tournament at Pebble Beach on the Monterey Peninsula.

Their relationship was friendly, but it had gotten off to a rocky start at Bing's office on the lot at Paramount Studios.

Murray arrived for an interview and was asked by Crosby's secretary to wait in an outer office, as Bing would join him shortly. Thirty minutes passed but Crosby hadn't showed. Jim began to worry and asked the secretary how much longer it would be. The woman went into Crosby's office to check, then returned and said it would be "just a few more minutes."

An hour dragged by and Murray, tired of waiting, told the secretary that he had a deadline and other appointments. The woman got up from her desk and opened the door. "Mr. Crosby, the man from *Time* magazine is still here." Murray heard Crosby say, "Fuck him!" It turned out he wasn't busy, he just wanted to make Jim wait.

"Crosby had the coldest blue eyes," Gerry Murray recalled. "If you tapped him on the shoulder, he would turn and look at you with a cold stare. But if he knew you, he'd warm up."

As he finished lunch, he talked about an interview with Marilyn Monroe when she was on the threshold of becoming a star in 1953. Jim picked her up at her apartment and drove to a restaurant on Sunset Boulevard for dinner. When the interview was over, Murray offered to drive her back home, but Marilyn said that a friend was coming to pick her up. Murray saw that Joe DiMaggio was in a booth at the back of the restaurant, so Jim said, "If I can't drive you home, can I meet your friend?" And she gladly introduced him to DiMaggio.

We had a cup of coffee and Murray paid the bill. I drove him back to Bel-Air and he asked me if I could take him to Anaheim Stadium the next day. The New York Yankees were in town to play the Angels and he wanted to interview Tommy John and Reggie Jackson before the game. Jim never said, "Pick me up tomorrow." He always said, "Can you pick me up tomorrow?" I said yes and would be there in the early afternoon.

Later that summer, Walter O'Malley died. Murray wrote: *"O'Malley changed more than the map of baseball. He changed the philosophy. The game will be poorer without him. Baseball is again at a crossroads and now there is no O'Malley to maneuver a steady hand across the shoals ahead. The talent is about to swallow the game whole as it did in Hollywood years ago. Aesop would have nodded wisely. The golden goose may not be long for this world."*

Chapter Three

REGGIE, LAZ AND YAZ

"A hot dog at the ballpark is better than steak at the Ritz."
—Humphrey Bogart

It was a long way from Murray's house to Anaheim Stadium, now Angels Stadium, at least 50 miles. You could drive to the Forum and Hollywood Park on the San Diego Freeway in 20 minutes from Bel-Air. Dodger Stadium was 25 with no traffic. But Anaheim Stadium was over an hour, with luck. In baseball, the visiting team arrived at the ballpark around four o'clock for a night game. That was the best time to interview the players because they were accessible. They hung out in the clubhouse, played cards or answered fan mail, and it was easy for the team's public relations department to set up an interview.

Jim said he used to make a day of it when he went to an Angels game. He'd drive to Anaheim in the late morning, get his car washed, then go over to the visiting team's hotel and have lunch. Sometimes, he might catch the player there and do the interview. Or, he'd get a room and take a nap. If he stayed for the whole game, he would go back to the hotel, then drive home the next day.

The traffic was light as we rode through Long Beach and over the L.A. County line into Orange County. Murray had a small silver tape recorder that he now used instead of a pen and notebook. It was the size of a pack of cigarettes and it had an attachment for a telephone so he could dictate to the transcription typists at the *Times*. The problem with a tape recorder was that his entire interview would frequently end up in the column. It included material that would have been edited out if he had composed it on a typewriter. A few of the *Times'* editors noticed this and their observations that Murray's column was running longer got back to Bill Shirley. The quotes that were never there were now sneaking in.

"If I could just see the words on the paper," Jim said as I drove into Anaheim Stadium's parking lot. And, in frustration, he added, "You know, with the way things are now, it isn't easy being funny."

It was one of the few times he complained about his predicament. And it was more a statement of fact than a complaint. I parked the Mustang and we walked to the Yankees locker room. Jim knew the way better than I did.

The Angels, tired of being tenants of the Dodgers and needing a fan base of their own, had moved to Anaheim when Orange County was a community of small towns, railroad whistle stops and citrus groves. Its biggest attraction was Disneyland. Now the area was a boomtown with real estate developments that included upscale housing and commercial buildings. Freeways had been expanded to handle the increase in automobile traffic. John Wayne Airport in nearby Costa Mesa had arrivals from and departures to destinations all over the western half of the United States. South Coast Plaza in Costa Mesa and Fashion Island in Newport Beach catered to the well-heeled denizens of Balboa, Newport Beach, Carlsbad and Irvine.

The Angels' cozy ballpark, built to seat 42,000, was about to be expanded for the arrival of the Rams, who would move south from downtown L.A. at the conclusion of the 1979 season. Since it opened, I had attended a few games at Anaheim Stadium, including an exhibition football game between the San Diego Chargers and Kansas City Chiefs.

We arrived at the entrance to the visitors' clubhouse and just as I reached for the doorknob, the door swung open and there stood Reggie Jackson, Mr. October. It almost seemed like he was waiting for us. Jackson greeted Jim warmly, but when Murray introduced me, Reggie turned, took him by the arm and walked away. I followed them to the middle of the dressing room and it hit me that I was in the locker room of the most famous team in baseball, the defending world champions who had beaten the Dodgers in the World Series the two previous seasons.

I looked around and tried to soak up the moment. There was catcher Thurman Munson, pitchers Ron Guidry and Jim "Catfish" Hunter, third baseman Graig Nettles, shortstop Bucky Dent, reliever Rich "Goose" Gossage, sluggers Chris Chambliss and Jim Spencer, and the manager, Billy Martin. They wore the classic Yankee road uniform, the solid gray pants and shirt with a slight tint of blue, and the simple yet perfect NEW YORK lettering across the chest.

I grew up an L.A. baseball fan, first rooting for the Pacific Coast League's Angels, with slugger Steve Bilko, and also the Hollywood Stars who had Dick Stuart, known as Dr. Strangeglove because of his erratic play at first base. The Stars were an affiliate of the Pittsburgh Pirates, and Stuart, who would go on to play 11 years in the major leagues, hit over 60 home runs one season for Hollywood.

Bilko and the Angels played in Wrigley Field, a scaled-down replica of the original in Chicago. Bilko spent much of his career in the minors but when he was called up to the big leagues, he played for the Cardinals, the Reds and the Tigers until he became a member of the American League's expansion Angels in 1961. When he hit a home run, the ball started out as a towering pop-up behind shortstop, and would then carry to the outfield and over the fence.

The first professional baseball game I saw was between the Stars and the Vancouver Mounties at Gilmore Field in 1956, and the weekend games between the Angels and Stars were always televised in Los Angeles.

Murray said the Yankees were more of a corporation than a baseball team. The owners were rich, they could afford the best players and it seemed that the Yanks were in the World Series every time you turned around. Jim said rooting for the Yankees was like rooting for U.S. Steel or IBM.

But I had a soft spot for them because their triple-A team, the Bears, played in Denver when my grandfather worked for the *Denver Post*. He sent me a real Yankees baseball cap, shoeboxes filled with used baseballs, and books and magazine articles on Joe DiMaggio, Mickey Mantle, Casey Stengel and Babe Ruth. A book on Ruth, written by Bob Considine, had a letter from Ruth to my grandfather pasted on the inside cover.

Murray told Jackson that he wanted to talk to him but he first wanted to visit with Tommy John. They arranged to meet on the field after Reggie had taken batting practice.

John, who had come to the Yankees after seven years with Dodgers, was having a superb season. The ground balls from hitters who swung at his marvelous sinker were being gobbled up by the Yankees' sure-handed infielders. He would win 21 games in 1979. What interested Murray more, though, was what prompted John to abandon the Dodgers and the paradise of sunny Southern California for the uncomfortable summer climes of the East Coast? Murray turned on his tape recorder and John, who stuttered slightly when he talked, said that he had asked for a new contract of three years, but the Dodgers offered only two. "Besides," he said, "the Dodgers didn't seem to want me. I wanted to go to a place where they appreciated baseball."

John pulled on his navy blue stirrup stockings then picked up his mitt and slapped the pocket with the back of his hand. "I could walk down the Sunset Strip as unnoticed as a tourist from Dubuque. In New York, I'm a celebrity, I'm a Yankee. In L.A., I was just a guy next door who kept such odd hours. In New York, the fans stay and cheer till long after the game. In L.A., everybody went home in the seventh inning, whether the score was tied or not."

Murray asked Tommy if he thought his departure was the reason the Dodgers were 15 games out of first place and in the NL West cellar. John responded, "Look, they traded away Rick Rhoden, Doug Rau came up with a torn rotator cuff and Terry Forster has been pitching hurt. Add those up and you come up with 46 to 50 games short the Dodgers are this year. Why lay all the blame on me?"

After 15 minutes, Jim ended the interview and thanked John, who as a member of the Dodgers had made a near-miracle comeback after he underwent a revolutionary surgical procedure that repaired the injured elbow of his pitching arm. We left the clubhouse through the tunnel that led down to the dugout.

The Yankees were taking batting practice and Murray suggested that we sit on the bench until Jackson had taken his swings. As we waited, I watched the ballpark fill up. The Yankees had loads of fans in Southern California and I remember going to a day game in 1965 between the Angels and Yankees at Dodger Stadium. Mantle, hobbled by injuries for most of his career, was healthy for a change and he started that day in center field. He gracefully shagged fly balls before the game, and fired perfect strikes to second base, third and to home plate. The sound of the ball hitting the catcher's mitt crackled like gunfire around the ballpark.

Frank Finch said that in 1951, the Yankees stopped in Los Angeles on a postseason tour to play the USC baseball team at Bovard Field on the Trojan campus. The writers brought stopwatches and timed Mantle running from home to first base out of the left-handed batter's box, in about three seconds. Finch said it was the fastest he'd ever seen anyone run, and Frank was used to seeing fast runners because he covered the Rams.

Another Mick, Mickey Rivers, would be in center field for New York on this night and a large number of the media had come out to the game because Nolan Ryan was pitching for the Angels. A few weeks earlier, Ryan had thrown his fourth no-hitter against the Baltimore Orioles, tying him with Sandy Koufax. Now he had a good chance to set the record of five because the game was to start in the twilight of five o'clock, and Ryan's fast ball would be difficult for the Yankee hitters to see at that hazy time of day.

Jackson finished his batting practice, but, instead of coming to the dugout, he grabbed his glove and ran to the outfield to play catch with the other outfielders. Murray began to worry because it was close to when the press had to be off the field. The American League's rule was strict: everyone out at 30 minutes before the first pitch. Jim wondered why Reggie was making him wait. He was doing a good imitation of Bing Crosby.

Finally, at 4:20 p.m., Jackson jogged in and sat down next to Murray. Jim turned on his tape recorder and they were cordial with each other for the remaining few minutes. A photographer took a picture of them on the bench, then Murray wished Jackson good luck. We left for the press box to have dinner and to watch the game.

The dining room outside the press box served a delicious buffet; prime rib was the entree. But Murray liked a hot dog or a hamburger from one of the concession stands. He said the best hot dogs at Dodgers Stadium were sold at the stand on the field level behind home plate. Anaheim Stadium had good hot dogs too, so we passed on the buffet.

There was a large contingent of Eastern writers traveling with the Yankees, and the press box was full. The Angel and Yankee beat writers got seats in the first row, but for everyone else it was Murray's Law: "Find a seat and sit down until somebody tells you to move." Buzzie Bavasi, the Angels general manager, graciously got Murray a chair near the front, and I sat in the row with the television and radio reporters.

As expected, Ryan was unhittable in the dusky twilight. From the press box, his fast ball was a speeding dot. Imagine what it looked like to the Yankee hitters. Reggie was asked once what it was like to face Ryan. "Every hitter likes fastballs," Jackson said, "just like everybody likes ice cream. But you don't like it when somebody is stuffing it into you by the gallon. That's what it feels like when Nolan Ryan throws fast balls by you!"

The Angels, though, were having their way with the Yankees' hurler Luis Tiant. They scored six runs off of the Cuban right-hander and Ryan breezed into the top of the eighth inning with his fifth no-hitter only six outs away.

But as it got darker and the lights brightened the field, the fastball became easier to see. First baseman Jim Spencer hit a sinking liner to center.

Rick Miller, as sure-handed an outfielder anywhere, raced in to catch it. He went into a slide on his left side and lunged out with his glove as far as he could. The ball grazed his mitt and kicked off to the green grass. The official scorer was Dick Miller of the *Herald-Examiner*, "Hoggy" to his peers, and he immediately ruled the play E-8, an error on Miller.

The Yankees jumped off their bench and stood on the top step of the dugout. Thurman Munson waved a towel, and others shook their fists and glared up at the press box. But what boos there were from the Yankee fans were drowned out by the cheers from the capacity home crowd because Ryan still had a chance to pass Koufax.

In the press box, however, the scene was chaotic. Bavasi ran toward Dick Miller, screaming, "How could you make such a stupid call." Then he made an unprecedented apology to the New York writers, who tried to get a quote from Miller on why he made his decision. Scott Ostler, who was covering the game for the *Times*, half-jokingly said to Murray, "Jim, even you could have made that call." Despite the uproar, Hoggy didn't waver. He stayed with E-8.

The game resumed and in the ninth inning, Jackson hit a sharp grounder up the middle into center field that ended Ryan's chance. He tipped his cap to Ryan when he stopped at first base. The hit also scored a run and the final was 6-1 Angels. The crowd cheered Ryan as he walked off the mound after the final out, and Jackson said, "I wish I could have given him a standing ovation myself, but I guess I would have looked a little foolish."

Of Jackson, Murray wrote: *"The thing Reggie Jackson has going for him is instant celebrity. He makes whatever he wants a Happening. He does not just go out and bash baseballs, and then retire reticently. Reggie trails a cloud of controversy, turmoil, uproar and unrest. He is the Bolshevik of the batter's box, the renegade of the locker rooms, the Robin Hood of right field.*

"You would never mistake him in the field for Joe DiMaggio. You would never mistake him at the plate for Lou Gehrig. If he played in Babe Ruth's era, the Babe would probably forget his name. But for the 1970s, Reggie was a child of his times. Like Babe Ruth, he seemed to come with a pennant attached.

"Reggie lights up scoreboards, and lives in a way Babe Ruth only dreamed of. He gets candy bars named after him not only because he is a star, but because he can act the part out."

It had been an exciting night and it made the trip back to Bel-Air pass quickly. Dan Hafner said later that he thought Dick Miller made the right call, that the general rule was that if a fielder gets his glove on the ball he should catch it.

Murray thought he found the reason why Jackson made him wait for their interview. When he listened to the tape of the conversation with Tommy John, there was a voice chattering in the background. It was Reggie talking across the room to John. "Hey, didn't you use to play with those Hollywood boys [the Dodgers]? You played with those Hollywood motherfuckers, didn't you?" Murray reasoned that Jackson was angry because Jim wouldn't first talk to him.

But what I remember from that night is seeing Thurman Munson stand on the top step of the dugout with his shin guards on, waving a towel toward the press box. A few days later, on August 2, the Yankees captain would be killed in a plane crash at an airport near Akron, Ohio. He had a pilot's license and was practicing takeoffs and landings in his private jet. It was a devastating loss to the Yankees because Munson was their leader, the heart of the team.

****

Of all the sports venues Murray visited, the most exciting and fun to be at were the racetracks at Santa Anita and Hollywood Park. An empty tennis court or a football stadium needs players and fans to come alive, a golf course is scenic but without golfers, a tree-shaded park is just as pretty. But a racetrack is a happening place, and it comes alive at six o'clock in the morning when the grandstands are empty, and continues until the late afternoon when it's post time for the featured race.

Murray had arranged to meet Laz Barrera, the trainer of Bold Forbes, the winner of the 1977 Kentucky Derby and Belmont Stakes, and also of Affirmed, the Triple Crown-winning wonder horse of 1978. We drove through Santa Anita's main gate, off Huntington Drive in Arcadia, at 6:30 a.m., and I parked close to the main grandstand where Jim was to meet Barrera. It was light, but a heavy marine layer, the kind that cools Southern California's summer mornings, obscured the majestic San Gabriel Mountains a few miles away. The Irish would have called it a soft morning.

Although Santa Anita was dark for the summer, the track still buzzed with activity. Horses went through hard workouts by exercise riders on the main track. Others were out for an easy gallop. Trainers kept close attention to stop watches and fragile legs.

Jockey Laffit Pincay, dressed in a full workout suit, jogged along the outside rail, sweating off the ounces to make his weight. He ran past a tempting array of pastries, coffee and doughnuts that was set on a table for anyone who wanted breakfast.

It was like this most mornings. Murray once interviewed Ron McAnally, the trainer of the rambunctious super gelding John Henry. He met McAnally and they walked from the track to the trainer's barns on the backstretch. John Henry, who twice was named Horse of the Year and had won more money (39 wins in 83 starts for $6.6 million) than any horse in history, had had a workout that morning, a cool-down walk and a bath. His grooms had put him in his stall and he hung his head out the door as Murray and

McAnally approached his hay-and-straw-carpeted palace. One of the grooms, a young Latino boy, had a bucket of carrots and he fed a couple to John Henry. I asked him if I could give him a carrot and the groom let me take one. I offered it to John Henry and he chomped it down. I reached for another one, but the boy said, *"No más, no más!"*

Suddenly, the horse got a wild look in his big brown eyes and he reared up on his hind legs. He snorted and shook his head. He wanted another carrot, but the groom took the bucket and walked away. It's well known that thoroughbreds are one of the most pampered and spoiled of all animals. John Henry rose up again and slammed his head on the stall's crossbeam. But McAnally, who was used to the horse's tantrums, casually opened the gate and he and Murray went inside. I was worried for Jim's safety, but when McAnally patted John Henry on his neck, the horse calmed down.

We waited for Barrera near the rail on the grandstand side of the track. The silver-haired Cuban eventually arrived from the direction of the barns with one of his sons, who also was a trainer. He apologized for his tardiness and said that he had an emergency with a horse that he had stabled across town at Hollywood Park. He asked if the interview could be rescheduled, and he and Murray arranged to meet at the Inglewood track the next day, in the Turf Club for lunch. Jim told me to wear a jacket and tie because the Turf Club had a dress code.

Murray was a reluctant celebrity at the track. He enjoyed hanging out in the paddock, where he could watch the horses being saddled, and also talk to the jockeys and trainers. People would call out to him as he walked from the paddock to the press box, and Jim would modestly acknowledge them with a wave and hello. He wasn't a big bettor but he would buy a tout sheet for $5 and it seemed he always cashed more than one ticket before the last race was over.

Marge Everett, the owner of Hollywood Park, was among an inner circle of Murray's friends, a social loop that included columnist Jack Smith, *Times* editor Bill Thomas, Murray's lawyer Paul

Caruso, Rams general manger Don Klosterman, Rams' physician Dr. John Perry and jockey Bill Shoemaker. The next day, Everett waited outside the press box elevator. She had heard from the track's PR office that Jim was coming and she was concerned about her friend's blindness. As we rode the elevator to the press box, Jim gave her an update on his condition.

We met Barrera for lunch. It was a special day for him because Affirmed was at the track to parade between races, the equine version of a farewell tour that legendary two-legged athletes take before they retire. I mentioned to Jim on the freeway that I had heard Affirmed's jockey, Steve Cauthen, say in a television interview that Affirmed was the most courageous horse he had ever ridden. He said that when Alydar, Affirmed's gutty rival in the Kentucky Derby, the Preakness and Belmont Stakes, tried to pass him in the stretch, the chestnut colt "dug in" and would not let Alydar by. I waited for Jim to say something but he was silent.

Murray interviewed Barrera as we ate. Jim used his tape recorder and I took notes. Later he wrote, *"They have yet to make the horse Laz Barrera couldn't teach to talk if he had the proper amount of time,"* and recalled the trainer's near-miracle work in getting Bold Forbes ready to run in the Belmont Stakes after the colt had been kicked in the hoof by Honest Pleasure coming out of the gate in the 1977 Preakness. *"The hoof looked like a piece of steak tartar,"* Murray noted in his column.

Jim recounted how Barrera had bucked the Kentucky and East Coast racing establishments by training his horses in California. The critics generally dismissed horses from the West Coast and predicted Affirmed would fail because Barrera had let him run in the Santa Anita Derby and the Hollywood Derby instead of bringing him early to Kentucky to train at Churchill Downs.

Laz had the last laugh, though, saying, "How does a horse know he's in Kentucky? Besides, you people act like California were in China. It isn't, it's in America."

53

Murray wrote, *"In his only race in Kentucky, Affirmed brushed aside Alydar in the stretch, saying 'Sorry old boy, this is for members only,' and won by an easy length and a half.*

"Laz Barrera sat in the press box the other day and watched as Affirmed paraded between races. 'He is not only the best horse I ever trained, but he is the most intelligent.' It seems kind of unfair. Not only can he run faster than humans, he can probably spell better."

As we were leaving, Marge Everett caught up with Jim, took his arm and walked him all the way out to the car. Her kindness and how much she thought of Murray impressed me. A few days later, Jim unexpectedly said, "I think what you said about Affirmed the other day is really true." I reminded him that it was Cauthen who said it but he wanted to talk about it again. The Affirmed-Alydar races became one of our favorite topics of conversation.

****

A few days later, Jim, accompanied by Gerry, flew to Boston to see eye specialists at the city's General Hospital. He had consultations with Dr. Richard Krantz, a cataract surgeon, and Dr. Charles Scheppens, a renowned retinal surgeon, whose list of patients included singer Ella Fitzgerald, actress Lauren Bacall, actor Jason Robards and Angels owner Gene Autry. Jim had hoped the doctors would approve the removal of the cataract. But they told him it was a risky surgery because that retina could detach too. The doctors would wait until the cataract was "ripe" before a decision was made.

But, Krantz gave Jim an optical device that looked and worked like a small telescope. He asked Murray to try it the next time he went to a baseball game. At the end of the exam, Murray asked the doctors when they would know when the cataract would be mature enough to take off. Krantz said, "You'll know when it's ready."

While in Boston, Murray, on a chance, wanted to interview

the Red Sox's superstar Carl Yastrzemski, who was attempting to become the first player in American League history to collect 3,000 hits and 400 home runs. One of the few things on the East Coast that Jim still had a soft spot in his heart for were the Red Sox, the team he rooted for as a boy growing up in New England. Jim was such a fan he named one of his sons Ted, after Hall of Famer Ted Williams.

But the Sox had ended a home stand and had left town for games in the Midwest. So, Murray decided to look up Yastrzemski when the Red Sox visited the Angels later in the summer.

Carl was about to turn 40 and, as a player, this would probably be one of the final opportunities to see him. The Red Sox still had the nucleus of the team that played the Cincinnati Reds in the thrilling 1975 World Series, with Yaz, Fred Lynn, Jim Rice and Bernie Carbo on the roster, but as the season headed into August, Boston trailed the Baltimore Orioles and the New York Yankees in the American League's East by several games.

Murray had a saying: "Just when they say hello, it's time to say goodbye." He was referring to players such as Roberto Clemente and Ted Williams who avoided giving interviews or had prickly relationships with the press when they were in their prime, but, as their careers headed toward the day they wouldn't put on the uniform again, would warm up to the media. The change of heart usually came when the player realized that it would be easier to get a job as an announcer in television and radio or be hired to endorse a company's soft drink if they cooperated or even smiled once in awhile. Steve Garvey, O.J. Simpson, Joe Morgan and Magic Johnson had this figured out from the start. But players such as Dave Kingman, who once dumped a bucket of ice water on a reporter's head, Rod Carew, who would go for games without talking to beat writers, and Kareem Abdul-Jabbar, who would turn his back on newsmen when they tried to get quotes after a Lakers game, never did.

Murray said Williams was temperamental, even if he had a good day at the plate, which for Ted Williams was most days.

Writers would ask about a certain play and he would shout, "Get away from me." So, they would go to another player and ask him the same question. The player would start to answer and suddenly Williams would jump in and yell, "No, no, that's not what happened. Here's what happened!"

Carl Yastrzemski, Williams' successor in Boston, was a loner and had a temper too, and he could be aloof and distant. When Jim finally caught up with him in Anaheim, Yaz insisted that he first be allowed to eat his dinner, in private.

Murray waited outside a small room in the Red Sox's clubhouse where the groundskeepers stored brooms and rakes. After a few minutes, Jim slowly pushed the door open and there was Yaz sitting on a table in a T-shirt and shorts, eating food from a paper plate. "I'll be finished in a minute," he said.

It was another 10 minutes before he came out of the storeroom to talk. Jim later wrote, *"It's hard to realize it now but Carl Yastrzemski was not always the toast of New England."*

"The fans expected another Ted Williams," Yastrzemski told Jim.

"Something I never was and never could be—and neither could anyone else. The man was the greatest hitter who ever played the game. The difference in size, for one thing. He was a big, strong power hitter. I could hit with power but not the power of a Ted Williams."

Yastrzemski even turned back the captaincy of the Red Sox in 1966. "I was too young for that responsibility," he explained. "I had enough pressures on a youngster."

"In Boston, they're no longer looking for another Ted Williams, they're looking for a new Carl Yastrzemski. And if another precocious youngster does make the Red Sox chain, the fans will be derisive as usual.

"'Call yourself the new Yastrzemski, do ya?!' they will jeer. 'Lemme see ya win a World Series! Why, you ain't even a new Ted Williams!' As for the one, the only, the original Carl Yastrzemski, he says only that he will have a two-word piece of advice for that youngster. 'Be yourself.'"

56

On September 12, Yaz singled off Jim Beattie of the Yankees for his 3,000th hit. He retired in 1983, saying that he loved baseball and the competition but "I never had any fun. I never enjoyed it. All hard work all the time."

Chapter Four

MURRAY STADIUM

"How can you write a column if you can't see the fucking game?"

—Pete Rose

The Murrays returned from Boston and Jim called to ask if we could go to Dodger Stadium. He wanted to see Tom Lasorda and Pete Rose before a game with the visiting Philadelphia Phillies. I arrived at the house at 3:30 in the afternoon and while I waited in the family room, Gerry came in and asked me to come into the kitchen. She closed the door and I could tell something was wrong.

She said when the doctors told Jim that the removal of the cataract on his right eye could cause the retina to detach, he became very dejected. He realized he'd be completely blind, and the idea had sent him into depression.

"Yesterday he was walking around the house, wearing an old sweater, all bent over like an old man," Gerry said. "And I yelled at him, 'You straighten up and stop feeling sorry for yourself. I never want to see you like that again.'" Her voice cracked and tears were in her eyes. She told me to tell her if I ever saw Jim that way. I heard Murray walking through the family room and he opened the kitchen door. He was sharply dressed in dark slacks, a light-blue sports jacket, white shirt and a tie. He asked, "Are you ready, Scheib?" As we left, I squeezed Gerry's arm, and told her not to worry.

Jim was silent as we rode on the Santa Monica Freeway toward downtown.

I wasn't sure what to say, so I asked him if he wanted to listen to some music. He asked me what kind. I had albums on cassette tapes by the Rolling Stones and the Who, but I didn't think he would want to listen to rock. I also had two Broadway shows, *My Fair Lady* and *The Music Man*. I said, "How about *The Music Man*?" Murray said, "Oh, I love Broadway musicals." I put it on and his mood brightened considerably. "You get two or three good songs and you've got a hit show," Jim said, as we swung onto the Harbor Freeway and headed north to the Third Street off-ramp.

Jim proclaimed that he was never unhappy in a ballpark, so I was glad we were going to Dodger Stadium, the first of many trips to Chavez Ravine.

Sometimes he would ask me what I knew about the visiting team. "Who's good on the Padres?" and I would say "Ozzie Smith." "I wrote about him last year," Murray said. Or, "Who's good on the Cardinals?" "Keith Hernandez!" I answered. "I don't know him that well," Jim said as he thought about the St. Louis first baseman. Once Murray asked me what I knew about Jerry Reuss. I said the Dodgers' left-hander reminded me of a Viking with his long blond hair and Nordic looks. I said I could see him with a sword and helmet with horns sticking out the sides, wearing a fur vest and leggings.

Murray said, "Don't stop, Scheib. You've got half the column written."

On this hot August evening, Murray would see two people whom he had written many columns about, sometimes more than one a year—Tom Lasorda and Pete Rose. I drove up Elysian Park Avenue and through the press gate to Lot B, the parking lot on the hill that had a great view of downtown Los Angeles. We parked next to catcher Steve Yeager's brown-and-gold Rolls Royce. An usher said hello to Jim, and he held the door of the elevator open for us. The car's operator took us down to the lower level where the clubhouses were located. The air was cool under the stands. We showed our press passes to a guard and entered the Dodgers' clubhouse. It felt like I had walked into the sanctuary of a church. The room was painted a brilliant white, the lockers gleamed against a plush royal blue carpet. The uniforms, washed and neatly pressed with the "Dodgers" script written across the chest and the red number underneath on the left side, hung just on the inside of each cubicle.

Jim sought out Nobe Kawano, the Dodgers' clubhouse attendant. Nobe always wore a T-shirt that said "You Be Happy" on the front. "Mr. Murray!" a voice called from the far end of the room. It was Don Sutton.

"Mr. Sutton," Jim called back, recognizing Sutton's Alabama drawl.

Now, with just a hint of a spring in his step, Murray walked into Lasorda's office, a spacious room just outside the clubhouse. "Da Manager" as Jim called him, sat at his desk, dressed only in his underwear. "Jim Murray," Tommy shouted. He jumped up and shook Jim's hand and slapped him on the shoulder. Then he took his arm and led him to a chair. So far, the year had not been a good one for Lasorda either. After guiding the Dodgers to the National League pennant in back-to-back seasons and World Series appearances against the Yankees, he found his team now foundering in last place, far behind the front-running Cincinnati Reds in the National League West.

Before a game, Lasorda's office, which was larger than the one of his predecessor, Walter Alston, was usually standing room only for Hollywood's elite players. Gene Kelly, Don Rickles, Peter Falk, Danny Kaye, Chuck Connors and Gregory Peck were pregame regulars. Frank Sinatra, Lasorda's good friend, would stop by regularly. But on this day, the only celebrities in sight were the pictures on Lasorda's wall.

Hollywood seldom backed a dud at the box office, or one on the baseball field.

Jim said he'd gotten a phone call from Connors, who starred in the 1950s TV western *The Rifleman* and had briefly played first base for the Dodgers and the Chicago Cubs before he became an actor. Connors generously offered to drive Murray to a game. "I'll pick you up at seven," Chuck said. Murray told him he needed to be at the ballpark at 4:30. "Four-thirty!?" There was a pause, and then Connors said, "OK, four-thirty, then we can leave in the seventh inning?" Jim told him, "No, I might have to stay until the game's over. If there's a no-hitter or somebody hits four home runs, I'll have to go to the dressing room, and then write." The offers from Connors and others suddenly disappeared. For a journalist, covering a big league baseball team was an 8-hour-a-day job, 7 days a week.

Jim introduced me to Lasorda and I sat down on the bench in his dressing cubicle. Tom sat back down in his chair with a weary look on his face. He ran his hands through his graying hair.

"God is testing us, Jim," he said. "He's testing you and he's testing me." He tried to sound upbeat, saying there were eight weeks left in the season and his team still had a chance to get back into the pennant race. But realistically, the season was over for the Dodgers. Sutton would win only 12 games, Burt Hooten 11 and Reuss just 7. Steve Garvey had a decent season, batting .315 in 162 games with 28 home runs. But Dusty Baker hit only 23, down from the 30 that he had hit in 1977 when he was one of four Dodgers to hit 30 or more home runs.

The team would finish in third place in the NL West, four games under .500, and attendance would slip under the O'Malleys' coveted 3-million mark.

Murray sympathetically wrote, *"But the other night, the one-time toast of Broadway, the dandy of the Burbank TV lots, was sitting in his underwear, his T-shirt read 'Please Don't Feed the Manager.'"* The last sentence of the column uniquely applied to both men: *"When the going gets tough, keep your shoes shined, keep your suit neatly pressed, even if it's your last one, put a carnation in your buttonhole every morning, even if you have to charge it, and show up at your favorite table everyday looking big."*

As Murray and Lasorda finished, Bill Russell, the Dodgers' shortstop, came into the room. He walked over to a table that was laden with cold-cut sandwiches, cheeses, chips, beer and soft drinks. Russell, the sandy-haired farm kid from Kansas whom Walter Alston brought in from the outfield to play shortstop, then stuck with him through criticism and boos directed at his error-filled play until Bill became an All-Star and a pillar in the Dodgers infield, helped himself to a snack. "Bill, you know Jim Murray?" Lasorda asked.

Later in the season, Murray wrote a column on Russell and his errors.

"Get out the Baseball Encyclopedia, Scheib, and look up His Honor, Johann 'Honus' Wagner, the Dutchman." He pointed out that the great Wagner, the shortstop who John McGraw said was the closest thing to the perfect player, had made 60 errors during the 1905 season. Jim added that Alston thought Russell could get to balls that other shortstops couldn't. When Murray did a column on an athlete, it was recognition that he or she had reached the top, that they were among the best in their sport. Russell was grateful as he sought out Murray in the clubhouse one afternoon, saying, "Thanks for the article, Jim."

Murray said goodbye to Lasorda and we left.

As we walked down the tunnel to the dugout, Murray said that even though he liked Lasorda and had known him since he was a minor league manager and a coach for the Dodgers, he didn't want it to appear that they were chums.

"You can't become friends with these people," Jim said, "because someday you might have to knock them." Bill Shirley had similar advice for his writers and copy desk editors. "We wish them well, but we do not root for them," was his motto.

Jim, however, said, "We do root for leads," which meant writers will pull for the team that's ahead to win because they want time to write a good story and make deadline. When it looked like Nolan Ryan might get his 5th no-hitter against the Yankees, the writers in the Anaheim Stadium press box were openly rooting for him because he was writing their game story. "Nolan Ryan, aided by a scorekeeper's controversial call, tossed his fifth career no-hitter Friday night against the New York Yankees, breaking the record he shared with Hall of Famer Sandy Koufax." What they didn't want was for something to happen that killed their angle. Fortunately, when Reggie Jackson broke up the no-hitter and knocked in a run to spoil the shutout, the writers still had a lead. They rooted for the Jackson angle. What they didn't want was a Yankee comeback that would send the game into extra innings.

I helped Murray up the steps of the Dodgers dugout and we walked onto the field. The Dodger starters took batting practice while the infielders ran down ground balls hit by coach Monty Basgall. Dodger Stadium gleamed like a jewel; its seats looked freshly painted, the blue outfield walls matched the color of the sky and the hills behind the parking lot were green and lush. The sound of bats hitting balls echoed around the field and the aroma of good smells was all around. Although he couldn't see it, Murray knew this scene well and I could see it made him feel better. Dodgers coach Preston Gomez, one of the nicest men in baseball, came up to Murray and asked how he was doing.

A wild throw from the infield almost hit us, so I positioned Murray safely behind the batting cage. Once in a while a ball would roll toward us and I would pick it up and throw it back. But on three occasions there was no one to throw it to, so I kept the balls and later got them autographed, by Pete Rose, Sandy Koufax and Nolan Ryan, when he later pitched for the Houston Astros.

Koufax had come to Dodger Stadium as a part-time instructor for the club's younger pitchers, and occasionally he'd throw batting practice. The Cincinnati Reds were in town for a three-game series and when Sandy took the mound, all the Reds players, some only half-dressed, stood on the top step of their dugout to watch. The young players were mesmerized as Koufax, his silver hair glistening in the sun, threw with his classic windup and delivery for about 30 minutes. His fastball still had velocity and the Dodger hitters couldn't wait to get in the batting cage. Afterward, Koufax saw Murray and walked over to him, and I got the ball signed.

Sportswriters have rules too: Two of them are no cheering in the press box and no asking of players for autographs. I was never a big autograph seeker. My grandfather had sent me a football signed by the *Look Magazine* 1956 All-American football team. Its signatures included those of Jim Brown, Paul Hornung, John Brodie, John David Crow, Leo Fischer, John Majors and Jim Parker. My friends and I signed the ball too, then we took it out in the street after school and played football. Autographs and baseball cards were everyday items in the 1950s and '60s.

We clipped Mickey Mantle and Willie Mays baseball cards with clothespins to the spokes of our bicycles or used them for bookmarks.

But this was too good an opportunity to pass up. I grew up listening to Koufax pitch on the radio. His Dodger team, with Don Drysdale and Maury Wills, was my favorite.

The batting cage was a good place to hang out before a game because players and managers from both clubs would congregate there and it was easy to talk to them. Once, at the World Series in Cincinnati, Murray was with a group of writers behind the cage and Jackie Robinson came by. Robinson, aged and nearly blind from a severe case of diabetes, approached Murray and said, "Jim, I wish I could see you." Murray replied, "No Jackie, we wish we could see you."

I noticed that a few of the Phillies had arrived, so we left the field through the gate behind home plate, walked past the concession stand that had Jim's "best" hot dogs and up the ramp to the visiting team's clubhouse. Some of the Philadelphia players had come to the ballpark early by cab and the rest would later ride the team bus. The visiting team was allowed less time for batting practice, so the Phillies dressed quickly and went out to the field to loosen up. Mike Schmidt ran laps around the warning track. In the visitor's clubhouse at Dodger Stadium, he was given the locker reserved for the Phillies' best player. It was located in a corner near the entrance to the showers. When the Pittsburgh Pirates were in L.A., it went to Willie Stargell; on the Giants, Willie McCovey got it; and during the 1981 World Series it went to Dave Winfield of the Yankees.

Pete Rose was probably Murray's favorite sports personality because he was a rarity—a great player who talked, who would express his opinion on just about anything, especially himself and the baseball records he wanted to break. Murray always asked the person he interviewed if they had any goals. Pete Rose had a lot of goals. To the writers, he was good copy. Jim said, "You ask Pete Rose a question, then stand back."

The Phillies had signed Rose away from the Cincinnati Reds for top dollar, $3.2 million, the highest contract at the time for a player in team sports. Rose said that Cincinnati, the team he was an eleven-time All-Star for in sixteen seasons, no longer wanted his services, but in reality the Reds lost a bidding contest to the Phillies. It paid off a year later when Rose would help lead Philadelphia to the National League pennant, and to the World Series against the Kansas City Royals.

Murray joined a small group of reporters that waited for Rose at his locker, about halfway down the row from Schmidt's. He didn't have to wait long. Pete came roaring in like a waterfront brawler into a bar, shouting expletives at his teammates, including Schmidt, who had just come in from his run. "Hey, dickhead, where were you last night?" Mike ignored the question, and as Murray and the others surrounded Rose, he changed from his street clothes into his uniform, put a red Phillies hat on his perfectly cut Prince Valiant-styled head of hair, and grabbed a bat, all in what seemed like 30 seconds. He gripped the bat as if he was strangling it, then someone asked what records he thought he had a chance to break.

The numbers tumbled out of Rose's mouth like a tape from an

adding machine. He already had his sights on Ty Cobb's all-time career hit record of 4,192, which he would break six years later. He also had calculated how many games he'd have to play per season to become the all-time leader in games played, and how many at-bats he would need to become the leader in the category of most seasons with 200 hits. Then he grabbed his glove and led the reporters, who were furiously taking notes behind him, down the tunnel and out to the field.

In a column later that week, Murray wrote, *"Pete Rose comes into a locker room like a kid on his way to a circus. Pete tears off his shirt and tugs his pants. He can't wait to get out of those mundane clothes and into a baseball uniform. You keep waiting for the rest of the parade. The elephants, the clowns, the breakaway cars. The prancing horses."*

Murray talked to Rose as he waited to take his swings in the batting cage.

"Pete, how's the adjustment going at your new position, first base?" He started to answer, then jumped in the cage. "Whack, whack, whack!" Three line drives, one to left, one to center and one to right. Then he was back.

"First base is no problem," he said. Rose had made the National League All-Star team as a first baseman that summer, his fifth All-Star position.

Rose knelt on one knee with his bat across his leg and he asked Murray how he was able to work with his eye condition. As Murray explained his situation and how he was managing to write his column, a wayward ball rolled my way and when Jim introduced me to Rose, I asked him to sign it. Then he was back in the cage again, taking more swings.

Murray knew Pete was no Eagle Scout, that he was a gambler and a womanizer, and although baseball looked the other way most of the time, Commissioner Bowie Kuhn had warned Rose about his betting and the unsavory gamblers he associated with. Jim said that Pete, who was married, had girlfriends in several National League cities. "The one in L.A. is the blonde that sits right behind home plate," Murray matter-of-factly noted. Despite Rose's transgressions, Jim staunchly supported him for election into the Hall of Fame, even after he was suspended from baseball for life by Bart Giamatti, because Murray believed Pete deserved the honor.

A bell in the visitors' dugout rang and it was time for the groundskeepers to take down the batting cage and get the field ready. Murray decided to head up to the press box. He said it was always a good feeling "to go home with a couple columns in your pocket." We usually exited through the gate on the field. But a few times the gate was locked, so we had to go back up through the visitors' dugout and out through their clubhouse.

Most teams didn't mind if a writer passed through before the game started.

Once Jim stopped to see Chuck Tanner, the manager of the Pittsburgh Pirates. In 1979, Tanner's team had sliced the National League East into pieces and his players, in their gaudy, yellow double-knit uniforms with the letters P-I-R-A-T-E-S in black across the front, were a band of scalawags. Jim made his way into Tanner's office, and I waited outside, thinking he would be just a couple of minutes. The clubhouse was a rambunctious playground. All-Star right fielder Dave Parker was putting a young bench-warmer in his place, lambasting the player for questioning Parker's decision on a play in a game the night before. "I make seven hundred and fifty thousand dollars a year," Parker shouted, slamming his hand on an equipment trunk. "How much do you make?"

Tanner appeared with Murray and he took Jim around the clubhouse and introduced him to each player. It was a classy moment. Suddenly the shouts stopped, and the room was quiet. Stargell, the gentle giant whom the Pirates called Pops, sat on the floor in front of the locker of honor. He slowly stood up and shook Jim's hand. "Mr. Murray." "Hello, Willie," Jim said.

Later, when I told Jim about Parker's outburst, Murray said, "John, when you see something like that, tell me right away."

The San Francisco Giants, on the other hand, were just the

opposite. It seemed their hate for the Dodgers also extended to members of the L.A. press.

Jim once stopped to talk to pitcher Vida Blue, and several Giants players took exception.

"Hey, get out of our clubhouse," yelled John Montefusco, a starting pitcher who was known as The Count. "Come on, Vida, you know the rules," another player said. But Murray and Blue went on with their friendly chat.

Another shouted, "Get the fuck out of here." I felt like saying, "Hey guys, it's Jim Murray, and he's blind." Darrell Evans and Willie McCovey knew Jim too but instead of telling their teammates to cool it, they kept quiet.

I said, "Come on, Jim, let's go." As we left, the Giants surrounded Montefusco like a football team would encircle a coach before a kickoff, and began chanting what they wanted to do to the Dodgers, most of which was unprintable. We escaped to the safety of the press box.

In the Dodger Stadium press box, Murray would invariably run into his good friend, broadcaster Vin Scully. "Hey, Murph," Scully would call. "Sully," Jim would reply.

The Western Union teletype machine clacked away, its spool of tape with line scores and updates from every game in the big leagues running down to the floor. We would usually sit in the front row, and on this night against the Phillies, Jim tried out his optical telescope. He peered through it and said he could see the home plate and the bases on the infield, but when the ball went into the outfield, he lost sight of it. I started then to give Jim a play-by-play of the game, telling him where the ball was hit. "That was a line drive into the gap, just out of the center fielder's reach." Jim said, "DiMaggio would have had it."

I also started to keep score because Murray would ask questions, such as, "What did Garvey do the last time up?" or "How many strikeouts does Seaver have?" or "What's the score?" That one once prompted a Murray lecture. I said, "The Dodgers are winning, three to two." Jim said, "Don't say a team is winning, or losing. The Dodgers are *ahead*, three to two, or the Phillies are *behind*, three to two." Jim explained that while the game was in progress, it was incorrect to say a team was winning or losing. The two words meant the game was already over.

Jim freely gave lectures, but he offered them in a kind way. Once I had forgotten my Dodgers press pass and we had to drive back to my apartment to get it. I hadn't cleaned the studio in over a week and there were dirty dishes in the kitchen sink. I told him the apartment was a mess and although he couldn't see, I was embarrassed for him to come in. Later, on our way to the ballpark, Murray said, "You know, your house is where you live." His point was that a cluttered apartment leads to a cluttered lifestyle. It was advice that I never forgot.

Each beat writer kept a scorebook that began with games in spring training and continued through the season. One night, Frank Finch asked Bob Hunter of the *Herald Examiner* to watch his scorebook while he went to the pressroom to get a refreshment, or as Frank called it, a Fillet de Coors. While he was away, Willie Davis made a spectacular catch in center field and Hunter noted the play with a "star" in Finch's book. Frank returned a couple of innings later, and when he saw the star he pointed to it and bluntly asked, "What's this?" Hunter said, "Oh, Willie Davis made a great catch." Finch paused, then said, "I'll be the judge of that."

The most memorable game I attended at Dodger Stadium with Murray was the night Fernando Valenzuela started his first game at home in June of 1981. It was at the rise of Fernandomania in Los Angeles, and Valenzuela, who had made his previous starts all on the road, was 4-0 coming into the game. His screwball had been compared to Carl Hubbell's and Latinos from East L.A. to San Fernando would attend games like never before. General Manager Al Campanis said the Dodgers were "blessed" to have Valenzuela.

The game against the San Francisco Giants was sold out and it was SRO in the press box. We found two seats in the last row and although it was hard to see the field because of all the bodies in front of us, at least Murray was in.

After Valenzuela retired the Giants in the first, second and third innings, he came to bat in the bottom of the third. Hitting left-handed, he lined a single to right. The roar from the crowd was the loudest I had ever heard, until a minute later when first base coach Manny Mota asked Valenzuela, in Spanish, to tip his cap to the crowd. Fernando hesitated, and Mota asked him again. He slowly took off the batting helmet and held it above his head. Six 747 jets couldn't have been louder.

Bud Furillo, a radio-show personality who had once been sports editor and a columnist at the *Herald-Examiner*, clamored over people in the next row to get to Murray. Furillo shouted, "Jim, Jim, we've got to protect him. We can't let happen to him what happened to Bo Belinsky." Belinsky was the L.A. Angels left-hander who in 1962 also started his rookie year with five wins that included a no-hitter against the Baltimore Orioles. But Belinsky was drawn to the bright lights of Sunset Boulevard and went to clubs on the Strip on nights before he was to pitch, usually with a starlet on his arm. His late-night escapades eventually caught up with his ability to get hitters out, and after Bo punched Braven Dyer of the *Times* in a Washington hotel room while the team was on an East Coast trip, the Angels suspended him and would eventually trade him.

Murray looked quizzically at Furillo, then turned his attention back to the game. It wasn't Murray's job to "protect" a player. He may write a column, for example, that encouraged officials at Augusta National to let black golfers such as Lee Elder and Charlie Sifford play in the Masters, but the Dodgers were capable of watching out for their prized Mexican pitcher.

Furillo's comment was a small illustration of the difference between the *Times* and the *Herald-Examiner* sports sections. Bill Shirley would never protect or promote an athlete. The idea would never enter his head. "We wish them well, but…"

Furillo was a fan. He wore a blue Dodgers jacket to games. Shirley rarely went to the ballpark. When he did, he'd stay until the 7th inning or ten o'clock, "whichever came first." Furillo frequented a bar in the L.A. suburb of Downey. Shirley had a glass of wine with his wife, Carol, at home after he left the office, which was at 6 p.m. on the minute. Bud was all over the L.A. sports scene, be it at fights at the Forum and the Olympic Auditorium, basketball games at the Sports Arena or football games at the Coliseum. Shirley half-bragged that he had never been to Pauley Pavilion and that he never met John Wooden. "Never met the man," he once boasted.

The *Herald*'s sports section catered to the hard-core sports fan and gamblers. It devoted plenty of space to horse racing handicapping, race charts and Las Vegas odds for all games, college and pro. The *Times* had one handicapper, Bion Abbott, and ran betting odds in a small box on the results page. Editorial space instead went to well-written feature stories that were aimed at the "thinking fan" and at the paper's upscale readers, especially those on the West side of Los Angeles, in Pasadena and San Marino.

Shirley was more interested in the people that played the games instead of the scores. The *Times* was located on a wealthy square block in the heart of the city's civic center. The *Herald-Examiner* building was about fourteen blocks south, in a less-than-desirable neighborhood. Once, Furillo came to work ecstatic, joyously announcing that the *Herald* had beaten the *Times* on a sports story. He giddily jumped around the office until Dwayne Esper, a track and field writer, said, "Bud, the giant up the street doesn't give shit what you do."

It was true. Shirley didn't blink at the local papers. He would get an invitation every year for the Associated Press' Sports Editors Convention, which was a week-long gathering of sports editors from papers across the country. They would judge contest entries in several categories including best beat writing, feature writing, column writing and makeup. Most of the judges were from smaller papers than the *Times*. Bill threw the invitation into the wastebasket. "I don't want Wayne Monroe [the sports editor of the *Pasadena Star News*] judging me," he sniffed.

Shirley considered *Sports Illustrated* his competition and he kept a wary eye on television, especially ABC and its highly-rated program *The Wide World of Sports*. Shirley envisioned his section as a paper-and-ink version of Roone Arledge's award-winning sports anthology show. Shirley sent Dwight Chapin to cover the 1972 Summer Olympics in Munich, the historic Games that brought Olga Korbut, Mark Spitz and the Black September terrorist strike against Israel's athletes onto a world stage. But one man, even as good as Chapin was, was little match against Arledge's division of seasoned TV professionals.

Dwight was a veteran, too. In the office, we called him The Dean. He had covered Wooden's basketball teams, McKay's Trojans and Prothro's Rams. And he wrote fast and accurately on deadline. But after about a week into the Games, Shirley called him at his hotel and said, "Dwight, ABC is beating us." Chapin was furious, and he fired back, "Then hire ABC, Bill," and hung up. Shirley didn't even worry about the big papers, such as the *New York Times* and the *Washington Post*, because in the 1970s, L.A. was a sports capital and the best writers and editors in the country were knocking on his door for a job.

It was Tuesday night, July 24, and the Dodgers routed Philadelphia, 15-3. The bats of Rose and the rest of the Phillies' had been muffled by Dodgers starter Burt Hooten, so after the fifth inning Murray asked me if it was all right to "go over the wall." It meant that he'd seen enough.

The month closed out with a trip back to the Forum where Jim interviewed a youthful Earvin "Magic" Johnson. The Lakers had brought their No. 1 draft choice from Michigan State out from the Midwest to play some games in L.A.'s summer basketball league, a six-week schedule between teams of first- and second-year pros. Johnson sat at a table in the Forum Club with two men in dark suits who were his agents. He drank two glasses of orange juice and barely spoke. He kept his head down through most of the interview and wasn't the smiling and gregarious Magic that basketball fans had seen when he led the Spartans to an NCAA championship against Larry Bird and Indiana State earlier that spring.

The agents answered most of Murray's questions. Finally, Jim asked Johnson directly, "Magic, do you have any goals?" He stared at his glass of juice, then said in a quiet voice, "All I wants to do is play bassaball." Murray was silent for a few seconds, then he turned and said, "John, do you have anything to add?" It caught me by surprise and the only thing I could say was, "No." Jim had never asked me to be a questioner in his interviews. I thought it was an intrusion and that the person he was talking to wouldn't appreciate it. It showed how thoughtful Murray was and I took it as a compliment. From then on I felt much more at ease around him.

In a column on Johnson later that week, Jim wrote: *"If all Johnson could do was grin, he would still be a welcome addition to the Lakers, but he did not get the nickname Magic sawing women in half, escaping from submerged tanks or pulling coins out of your ear. He acquired the sobriquet at a high school game once where he threw in 36 points, grabbed 19 rebounds, made 16 assists and tended to disappear from time to time. Magic is 6-8, 215 pounds. This is as good a trick as pulling an elephant out of a hat. Making a basketball disappear is at least as tough as a rabbit.*

"The nice part about signing Earvin 'Magic' Johnson is he brings the Los Angeles Lakers something they badly need—a smile."

AUGUST AND SEPTEMBER

Chapter Five

A CLOSE CALL

"Well, we saved the leg."

—Dr. Robert Wood

"What's happening in the real world, Scheib? What's going on down at the Great Religious Daily?"

These were questions that Murray would occasionally ask me when I went over to his house. In the real world in 1979, the Walkman was introduced by Sony; Margaret Thatcher was named the first woman prime minister of Great Britain; John Wayne died; the Soviets invaded Afghanistan; and the space probe Voyager II took pictures of Jupiter.

In baseball, Pete Rose broke Honus Wagner's National League record on August 5 with a single for his 2,427th hit; Walter O'Malley died at age 75 on August 9; Willie Mays was enshrined in the Hall of Fame; and Lou Brock collected his 3,000th hit on August 13 off Cubs' pitcher Dennis Lamp.

Summer had gotten "real" for the sports department, too. The Angels were in a pennant race, a position they hadn't been in since

75

1962. Gene Autry had brought Jim Fregosi home from warming the bench in Pittsburgh to manage the team in 1978. Fregosi had been Autry's favorite as an Angel player, and now his steady leadership, paired with the pitching staff anchored by Nolan Ryan and the hitting of Don Baylor and Brian Downing, gave the Angels a legitimate chance to win the franchise's first pennant. Also, the pro football training camps had opened and a few NFL teams had already played exhibition games. The Rams trained at Cal State Fullerton in Orange County and the Dallas Cowboys camped at Cal Lutheran University in Thousand Oaks. Jim had arranged with Doug Todd, the Cowboys' public relations director, to have lunch with quarterback Roger Staubach after the team's morning practice.

I gassed up the Mustang at a Texaco station at the corner of Barrington Avenue and Sunset Boulevard in Brentwood and we hit the road. The drive to Thousand Oaks took about an hour, but it was a pretty way to go, north on the Ventura Freeway (U.S. Highway 101), through rolling brown hills burnt by the summer sun. Horses and cows cooled themselves in the shade of tall oaks, and surfers from the San Fernando Valley, with surfboards strapped to their cars with towels and ropes, took canyon roads to get to the waves of Malibu and Santa Monica.

About five miles from the campus I noticed that my car's temperature gauge was creeping up to HOT, so I pulled into a shopping center parking lot and got out. I hesitated to look, afraid of what I might see, then peeked under the front end and saw a steaming green liquid trickling out of the radiator.

Fortunately, there was a drugstore there and I bought a gallon of antifreeze.

When I got back to the car, Jim was standing next to the door. "Is everything all right, John?" he asked. "I hope so," I said, praying.

Murray once had a lunch interview with horse trainer Wayne Lucas at a restaurant near Santa Anita. He said he knew where the restaurant was, that he had been there before, but when we got to the location, there was no restaurant in sight. We drove around the streets that backed up to the racetrack for over 15 minutes. As the time ticked by, Jim got more upset until he was swearing.

Finally we found the place, but he was uncustomarily late, which he hated.

Now, if the radiator didn't hold the new antifreeze, I would have to call somebody at the paper to come and get him. It would be touch-and-go for him to keep his date with Staubach because it was about 45 miles from downtown L.A. to where we were.

Fortunately, the motor cooled to normal as I drove on to Cal Lutheran and we made it ahead of time. I parked the car and as Murray got out, the Cowboys, in their white practice uniforms and blueish-silver helmets with the Texas Star on the sides, filed into the locker room. Staubach wore No. 12 on his jersey and he waved to Murray. Jim ranked the clean-cut leader of Big D among the NFL's all-time quarterbacks, in the top five.

Doug Todd waited for Murray and he took Jim into an office near the practice field. Inside were Tex Schramm, the president of the Cowboys, and Gil Brandt, the head of player personnel. The two men, along with coach Tom Landry, were the architects of one of the NFL's most successful franchises. They welcomed Murray and gave him a white golf shirt with the Cowboys logo on the pocket. Jim talked to them for a few minutes, then we followed Todd to the team's lunch room where we sat down at a long table, the kind you see in school cafeterias, with Staubach, a lone star on a team of stars.

Murray asked Roger about his decision to fulfill his obligation to the Navy instead of going into the NFL after he graduated from Annapolis in 1964.

Staubach, who won the Heisman Trophy as a junior in 1963, served in the Navy for four years, including a tour of duty in Vietnam. The Cowboys took a chance and drafted him anyway, even though they had Don Meredith, and later Craig Morton.

Staubach had worked out with the Cowboys while he was still at the Naval Academy and the Dallas hierarchy saw a future leader.

Roger thought about Murray's question as he ate, then said,

"If I had ducked my responsibilities then I would have spent the rest of my life ducking responsibilities." The rest of the interview was as straightforward; Staubach answered Jim's questions in crisp, military-like diction. He finished his lunch and thanked Murray, saying he had a meeting to attend before the day's second practice. The rest of the team had also finished lunch, so we walked out to the practice field.

The sea breeze was coming through the Santa Monica Mountains and it felt good on the warm day. There was a TV crew from the BBC on the sideline of the practice field interviewing linebacker Harvey Martin about the differences between American football and Europe's football—soccer. The British reporter, who had a facial resemblance to comedian Dudley Moore, put on Martin's football helmet, which was so big it fell over his eyes, and then asked the 6-foot-5, 260-pound defensive rock to demonstrate how a tackle was made in American football. Martin obliged by knocking him down with a swift forearm to the oversized helmet. The Brit's microphone went flying and those who had gathered to watch laughed, including Jim. Martin helped the reporter to his feet, brushed the dirt from his jacket and it took a couple minutes to get the wobble out of his legs.

Murray enjoyed British humor, Winston Churchill and the London theatre scene, saying once that he wanted to be a playwright but instead ended up a sportswriter. He did try his hand at screenwriting, working on the movie script on the life of Ben Hogan. In 1951, Hollywood made a hokey attempt to put Hogan's life on film with *Follow the Sun*, which starred Glenn Ford. Jim said the movie was written and produced by people who didn't know much about Hogan or golf. So, on a second attempt he was asked by Hogan himself to write the story, but the demands of producing a column five days a week left him little time to create a decent script. The old Hollywood axiom, "Do you want it good or do you want it by Thursday," repeatedly came into play, and the producer got another writer. The sports world, not Hollywood or Broadway, ended up the winner.

78

Jim once attended a fight at the Olympic Auditorium with his son, Ted. The bout was a bloody brawl between two welterweights and finally the younger Murray turned to his father and said, "How can you sit here and watch this?" Jim replied, "There's no better theater."

The Dallas assistant coaches ran the afternoon practice while Landry watched with his wife from a blue sedan parked on the far side of the field. The Cowboys relished the Cal Lutheran site because it was a perfect place for a summer football training camp, and the envy of several NFL teams. George Allen tried to wrestle it away from Dallas when he was the coach of the Rams. The weather was hot during the day, but not blistering. There weren't any big-city temptations to distract the players. After two-a-day practices, most of them just wanted to relax in their dorm rooms with a pitcher of beer, which the coaches let them have.

Later that week, Jim wrote: *"Roger Staubach found the Cowboys backfield as easy to make as Navy's. He found Coach Landry's calculus no more complicated than Naval Academy midterms, as soon, that is, as you figured the cosines of the angles, and pretty soon he was leading the Dallas Cowboys to their first Super Bowl win ever, in fact, their first big game win ever. He still looks like a Navy recruitment poster."* This win came in Super Bowl VI against the Miami Dolphins, and Staubach was named the game's most valuable player. He was at the helm when the Cowboys faced the Pittsburgh Steelers in Super Bowl XII and he also guided the team to four NFC championships.

I worried about the leak in the radiator all afternoon but I didn't see any antifreeze on the ground when we left Thousand Oaks. I drove cautiously back to Bel-Air and we made it without a problem. A mechanic replaced a cracked radiator hose the next day and when I got home from the garage, Murray called to say he wanted to go to the Rams camp at Cal State Fullerton. This would be another lunch with the team and interviews with offensive tackle John Williams and linebacker Jack "Hacksaw" Reynolds.

The Rams training camp had a more relaxed atmosphere than

the Cowboys,' not that the L.A. players had it easier—the Rams' two-a-day practice sessions were just as tough and they had to deal with something the Cowboys didn't—smoggy air that blew in a southwesterly direction from the city. But Ray Malavasi, the Rams coach, allowed those players who lived in the area to go home between the morning and afternoon practices. When we arrived, Reynolds had left to feed and walk his dog. So, Jim looked up quarterback Pat Haden in his room to talk about his possible participation in a golf charity event.

In 1979, Haden would start his fourth season as the Rams quarterback. Murray admired Pat, a Rhodes Scholar, because, like Roger Staubach, he played the game with savvy and intelligence. Jim once wrote, *"Patrick Haden found nothing particularly difficult about throwing a football. Nothing to be compared to the difficulties of Ciceronian Latin, for example, or the logical thickets of Aristotle or even Alexander Pope..."*

However, when Haden was a senior at USC, Murray's opinion of his playmaking wasn't quite so high. In the famous 1974 game against Notre Dame at the Coliseum, the Trojans fell behind the Irish, 24-0, late in the first half. The USC players had stumbled all over the field, dropped passes and gained few yards on the ground while the defense couldn't stop Notre Dame's precision attack led by quarterback Tom Clements.

At halftime, Murray leaned over to the *Times'* Mal Florence, who was covering USC that season, and said, "You know, this incestuous relationship between Haden and the McKays is hurting the team." Murray was referring to Pat's boarding with USC Coach John McKay and his family at their home, something he had done since Haden and John McKay Jr., his inseparable friend, were teammates at Bishop Amat High School. The Haden-to-McKay formula was one of the most famous pass-and-catch combinations in Southern California prep football history and when the two enrolled at USC, the senior McKay made it an integral part of the Trojans' offense.

But the second half was a complete reversal of the first. As one USC player said later, "We came out like madmen." Anthony Davis ran the opening kickoff back for a touchdown. On the following kickoff, the Trojans pinned the Irish on the 7-yard line, and the defense forced Notre Dame to punt. Then it was Haden to McKay, Haden to McKay, Haden to McKay, touchdown. USC scored 55 points in 17 minutes—on Notre Dame. This wasn't Utah State or Cal. The Irish were the defending national champions and had the top-ranked defense among Divsion 1-A schools. SC's comeback is still called the greatest in college football history. Murray, who referred to the Trojans as "the heathens" when they played Notre Dame, turned to Florence and, embarrassed, said, "I really gave you some good advice back there." Mal, who graduated from USC and covered the school's football and basketball teams throughout his renowned career, never let Murray forget it, and would bring it up at opportune times to needle Jim, prompting Murray to mercifully plead, "Hasn't the statute of limitations run out on that, Florence?"

Malavasi was a defensive coordinator under Chuck Knox and an offensive coordinator for George Allen, then became head coach when Allen was fired by Carroll Rosenbloom after two games of the exhibition season in 1978. He coached the Rams to a 12-4 season but lost to Dallas in the NFC championship game, 28-0.

Ray was known as a player's coach and was considered one of the top defensive strategists in the NFL. His best player was Jack Reynolds, the middle linebacker nicknamed "Hacksaw" because he supposedly once sawed an old truck in half after a loss for the Southeastern Conference championship when he was at the University of Tennessee.

Off the field, a simple composite of a football team would portray offensive linemen as conservative, straight-arrow guys, the leaders of the pack; wide receivers a cocky, yet easygoing bunch, boogalooing on the sidelines to their rock and soul music; quarterbacks the deep thinkers, studying their playbook as if preparing for a college exam; running backs the regimental soldiers, always staying in shape to keep their quickness. Linebackers, on the other hand, especially middle linebackers, didn't fit any of these profiles.

Instead, they are off in the corner like the toughs in the school yard, smoking cigarettes and plotting mayhem.

Murray approached the door of John Sumner Reynolds' room with the same caution as he did the time inside the Coliseum locker room when he knocked on the cubicle of Dick Butkus. The Rams had just beaten the Chicago Bears on a last-second field goal, 17-16, and Butkus was furious, growling on the other side of the door that a puny place-kicker who stood on the sidelines for over 59 minutes could come in and decide the outcome. As Jim slowly pushed the door open, he said he thought he could hear Butkus "licking his fur."

Reynolds tried to hide his intelligence behind a tough-guy persona. He didn't want anyone to think there might be more to him than being able to smash a fullback to the ground. He looked at Murray warily as the two sat across from each other. His eyes darted from Jim to me and then back to Murray.

Reynolds had led the team in tackles the previous season with 144, assisting on 83 and making 61 on his own. Ted Green, who covered the Rams for the *Times* in the late 1970s, said Reynolds had the uncanny knack to know where the ball carrier would go. "He'd run to the hole even before it opened and lay down and wait for the runner," Green said.

Murray asked, "Jack, can it be explained what you do primarily?" Reynolds grunted, then answered, "Sure, I protect the one and the zero hole, weak and strong." Murray wrote, *"And Hacksaw sat back triumphantly, as if he had explained 2 and 2 make 4."*

"See we have different fronts, the K.C. and the over and the under."

"The K.C.?" inquired Jim.

"Well, yes, of course, unless we're overshifted, don't you see? Some teams run to the weak side, you know."

Jim, a perplexed look on his face, paused for a second to gather himself.

82

"To be sure," Murray said. "Well, Jack, what do you do against the shotgun offense?" Murray asked.

"Well, we put in the nickel. Sometimes we put in six defensive backs, that's the dime. We've got to protect the bubble, or what I call the Mack," Reynolds responded. Jim said that he was "wishing the interview had subtitles."

"The bubble, the Mack?"

"Well, yes," said Hacksaw, "a quarterback will attack that, don't you see?"

"What about zones?" Jim asked.

"They'll flood the zone on us, of course."

Hacksaw was being Hacksaw, keeping the real Jack Reynolds out of sight.

Jim ended the interview feeling he had been talking to a football computer instead of a human being and later wrote: *"Don't expect Jack Reynolds to discuss great books or outstanding movies with you. Jack's idea of a great movie is a three-yard loss and the books he reads don't have dialog."*

We had lunch in the cafeteria and Murray sat with John Williams, the Rams' veteran offensive tackle. As Jim and Williams chatted, I watched the scene as the Rams came in and out of the cafeteria. The diminutive Haden strolled in, his shock of blond hair made him look more like a surfer coming in from a morning at Huntington Beach than an NFL quarterback. The team had him listed at 5 feet 11 inches and 180 pounds, but in person he looked shorter and lighter. Then there was defensive end Fred Dryer, who strutted around the room bare-chested, wearing only his blue Ram gym trunks. Dryer was one of the first players to advocate health food, such as fruits and yogurt, and mixing vegetables in a blender, as part of his training diet. After practice, Fred preferred carrot and celery juice to a beer. He looked more like a basketball player than a defensive end.

He was tall (6 feet, 6 inches) and lanky, weighing 240 pounds, almost anorexic for an NFL defensive end, and he was a free spirit who drove and even sometimes slept in a Volkswagen bus. The

Rams had acquired him from the New York Giants, who had made him their No. 1 draft choice out of San Diego State in 1969. He complemented Jack Youngblood, the Rams' other defensive end who was also strong against the run. What Dryer lacked in bulk he made up with quickness and speed. He used these assets to outmaneuver bigger men to get to the quarterback. He recorded two safeties in one game, against the Green Bay Packers no less, which is still an NFL record.

Murray and Williams were joined by Jack Teale, a Rams executive, and Jerry Wilcox, one of the team's publicists. Wilcox handled the print media and Jack Geyer, who once had worked as an editor in the *Times'* sports department, looked after the television and radio reporters. Geyer had a quick sense of humor and even wrote his own jokes. When the Rams were trying to think of a name for their new female cheerleader squad, Geyer had the winner in a snap, the Embraceable Ewes. Wilcox, a genuinely nice man, was troubled by liver and kidney ailments, and needed crutches to walk.

At Rams Park in Anaheim, where the team practiced during the regular season, Murray once visited Wilcox and general manager Don Klosterman. Don was a star football player at Loyola University in Los Angeles in the early 1950s.

Known as the Duke of Del Rey, Klosterman played one season for the Rams, in 1952, as a backup quarterback but had his football career shelved by a skiing accident. His injuries were so severe it was feared that he'd never walk again. It was a long rehabilitation until Klosterman could stand up. He had to walk with a cane and his stride was wobbly and unsteady. It was a sight to see Murray, who was blind, Wilcox on crutches and a teetering Klosterman make their way across the field three abreast. They looked like the famous painting from the Revolutionary War, *The Spirit of '76*. All they needed was a fife and a drum and a musket.

Jim said goodbye to Teale and Wilcox and decided not to attend the afternoon practice, saying he'd rather head home. Football practice was a lot like watching a movie being shot. The coach was the director and the players were the actors. He'd blow his whistle for "action" and again for "cut." If the coach didn't like what he saw, he'd make the players run the drill until they got it right. It was slow and tedious. Baseball and basketball practice sessions were much more lively. Football drills were comparable to sitting in a geometry class. A lot of teaching was involved, as the coaches explained what angles to take on tackles and pass routes. Eugene McCarthy, the senator from Minnesota who ran for president in the Democratic Party primaries in 1968, once said about football, "You have to be smart enough to understand it and dumb enough to think it's important."

We went out the back door of the cafeteria to a cement path that wound past the dormitories and ended at the parking lot. This part of the school was serenely landscaped with tall pine trees and a picturesque greenbelt that separated the buildings. The sun had gone over on the other side of the cafeteria, which left the walkway in heavy shade.

Jim always had me walk a couple of feet in front of him because he could see my outline. He didn't like me to guide him by the arm, but I should have done this one time. In the dark shade, he stepped off the walkway and crashed his left shin against a rusty sprinkler pipe. It tore a long gash in his right leg and he nearly fell. I reached back and helped him onto the walkway. He gasped in pain and had to stand still for a minute before he took a step. We got out into the sunlight and I could see a tear in the cloth and blood on his pants.

I suggested we find one of the team's trainers to look at the cut. Jim agreed and he limped to the practice field where we fortunately found George Mennefee, the Rams' head trainer. Mennefee said the wound didn't look too bad. He cleaned it with an antiseptic and put a large Band-Aid on it. He then wrapped it tight in an Ace bandage. George meant well, but he was treating Jim like a player. Tape him up and get him back into the game. What Jim needed was a real doctor.

I felt terrible as we rode back to Murray's house. I never

expected anything like this to happen and I blamed myself. I should have seen the pipe.

He didn't need another physical ailment. I dropped him off and he let himself into the house. I figured that was it for me, I was through working for him. Bill Shirley would be calling the next day and I'd be permanently back on the night clerk desk.

A week went by and I did not hear from Murray. I called his house but there was no answer. I found out later that he kept Mennefee's wrap on for three days. In that time the cut had become badly infected. Gerry took him to see Dr. Robert Wood, one of the Dodgers' physicians. Wood treated the leg and told Murray to keep it elevated and to walk on it only when he had to.

Finally, Jim called to say his leg was better, that he was on antibiotics, and could I come over and help him look up some statistics for columns on Lou Brock and Fred Lynn? Brock had gotten his 3,000th hit and Lynn, the smooth-as-silk outfielder for the Boston Red Sox, was having the best season of his career, slugging 42 doubles and 39 home runs, and hitting .333.

Murray wrote, *"The thing about Fred Lynn is that he's the only guy in the game who looks as if he might have arrived at the park via family chauffeur.*

"They let him play because he owns the ball, or his dad bought the uniforms. He looks more like the coxswain of the Harvard eight than one of the most feared sluggers in the American League. He plays the game with a ballet-like precision and grace, as if it were something scored by Tchaikovsky. His hat never flies off, he never falls down swinging at the ball and plays the game like an Englishman plays polo."

What a relief it was for me that Murray was better, and at lunchtime we drove to Love's Barbecue. In the restaurant, Jim took a key chain out of his pocket. It had a dog's tooth on the end of it. Jim said it had been given to him by Richard M. Nixon, when Nixon was a candidate for vice president on the 1952 Republican ticket with Dwight D. Eisenhower. *Time* magazine asked Murray if he'd like to take a break from the Hollywood beat to cover politics, and Murray picked up Nixon's campaign trail in the Pacific Northwest just as candidate Nixon was being accused of receiving payoffs, about $18,000, from a secret slush fund set up by his supporters to help underwrite his campaign.

Reports flew that Eisenhower would replace him if he didn't clear himself of the charge. This prompted Nixon to give his famous "Checkers" speech on national television, the address in which he said he was "as clean as a hound's tooth."

The speech was to be given on September 23, 1952, which was after *Time*'s deadline for that week, but Murray managed to persuade Nixon's publicist, James Bassett, who would later become an associate editor at the *Times*, to tell him in advance if the senator from California was on or off the ticket. In the press car of Nixon's train, Bassett took Murray aside and quoted some text from the speech. Murray concluded from what Bassett read to him that Nixon would not quit.

After Jim wrote his story and *Time* went to press with it, a wire service bulletin broke that said Nixon would indeed step aside and the report put Jim into a sweaty panic. He went back to Nixon, who annoyingly assured him that he had the story right. Murray was perplexed until he found out the wire story was erroneous. Murray and the other newsmen who had traveled with the future vice president were given the hound's tooth key chain as a souvenir of the campaign.

After lunch, Jim had a doctor's appointment for his leg, so we drove to Dr. Wood's office in West Los Angeles. As he entered the waiting room, Emmett Ashford, the major league's first African-American umpire, came out with his wife. Ashford recognized Jim and said hello. He did not look well, his dark skin was more gray than brown. It was announced later that his umpiring career was on hold because he had been diagnosed with cancer.

Murray saw Dr. Wood and when he came out of the examination room he didn't look good either. Jim's leg had healed, but when he thanked Wood for all that he had done, the doctor said, "Well, we saved the leg." It wasn't a joke. The problem was that Murray couldn't see the festering wound.

He limped painfully around on the leg until it was almost too late.

On future trips to Fullerton, Jim made a point to walk down the path and kick the sprinkler pipe with his foot, and afterward, like Mal Florence at the USC-Notre Dame game, picked his spots, usually when we were with a group of sportswriters or his cronies, to say, "Don't let Scheibe lead you down a shady path in Fullerton. He'll run you into a rusty sprinkler." The statute of limitations never ran out on that one.

Reggie Jackson was one of Murray's favorite interviews. Here, he visits with the Yankees' slugger near the batting cage in Anaheim. In a column on Jackson, Jim wrote, "...For the 1970s, Reggie was a child of his times. Like Babe Ruth, he seemed to come with a pennant attached."

Jackson and the Angels' Don Baylor pose with a fan for photographers at Anaheim Stadium. Baylor was the American League's Most Valuable Player in 1979, leading the Angels to the AL West title.

Members of the *L.A. Times'* sports copy desk staff surround Chuck Garrity, seated center, as they put together the paper on a busy college football Saturday. From left: John Cherwa, Larry Stewart, Garrity, Harley Tinkham, Jim Coontz and Avrum Dansky.

Tinkham and Dansky check a story for accuracy. Harley, who was known as "Ace," was a high jumper on USC's 1943 national champion track and field team; Avrum, below, played basketball at Marshall High School and graduated from UCLA. He kept up-to-date records on every player in Major League Baseball and the NBA.

Mal Florence, foreground, with broadcaster Roy Firestone, watches the conclusion of the 1980 USC-Notre Dame game from the sidelines at a packed L.A. Coliseum. Below, Florence, who covered both USC and UCLA football during his distinguished career, waits with a group of writers outside the Trojans' dressing room.

Although Pete Rose had moved on to Philadelphia, Cincinnati still had the nucleus of the famed Big Red Machine in 1979, with Ken Griffey, above, George Foster and Dave Concepcion, who take batting practice at Dodger Stadium. The Reds won the National League West but lost to the Pittsburgh Pirates in the playoffs.

Gerry and Jim Murray in February, 1983. Murray often said that
Gerry and his column were his lifelines during his blindness.

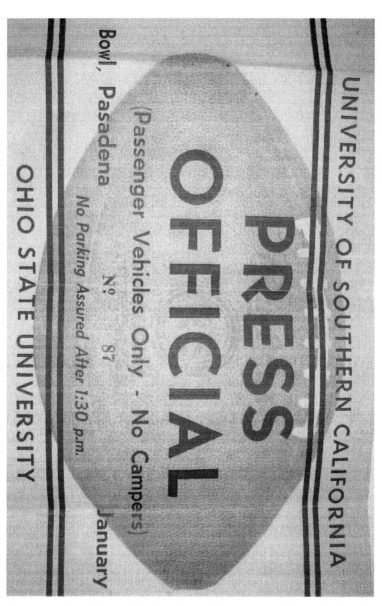

A sportswriter's best friend—the parking pass. This one is for the
1980 Rose Bowl, played between Ohio State and USC.

After he lost his eyesight, Murray used a tape recorder instead of a pen and notebook at his interviews. Here, he talks to Reggie Jackson in the dugout in Anaheim.

Chapter Six

THE SCOUNDRELS

*"The world is made for people who aren't
cursed with self-awareness."*
—Annie Savoy, from the movie, *Bull Durham*

There were cars parked in Murray's driveway that I had never
seen before.

It was the first Sunday in September and we were going to the
Rams' season opener at the Coliseum against the Oakland
Raiders. I also had brought Jim's mail, which would collect in the
sports department at a fairly fast rate. Marilyn White usually went
through it first then put what she thought Jim would want into a
cardboard box. It consisted of books and magazines, press
releases and letters.

I would carry the box into the kitchen and Murray would sit in
front of a trash can. I'd open each piece and read it to him, then
he'd either keep it or toss it away. Most of the letters were from
readers but one or two came from people Jim didn't like, usually
complaining publicists, which prompted him to say, "He's a prick,"

his favorite word for someone he didn't care for. The letter would sail into the trash. The books and magazines, though, always stayed. "Let's see what's in Sporty Illustrations," he'd say of his former employer, especially if there was a story written by his pal Dan Jenkins.

The Santa Ana winds whipped about and although it was hot and dry, there was a touch of fall in the air. Murray let me in and I could hear voices in the family room. Gerry was away in Michigan to visit her brother, Rodney Brown, who was ill. I walked in and there were three men engaged in a lively conversation. Lying on the couch was Will Fowler, at the bar was Don Page and swinging a golf club in the middle of the room was Bob William. These were three of Jim's best friends, but you would never find them among the inner loop who socialized in Marge Everett's penthouse.

Fowler was a former colleague of Murray's at the *Examiner* in the 1940s.

He was a police reporter who distinguished himself by his coverage of the brutal murder of a young Hollywood socialite named Elizabeth Short. The case was called the Black Dahlia Murder and it was never solved by the police. Will stepped up from the police beat to the publicity department at 20th Century Fox studios. He was a friend of W.C. Fields, whom he called Claude, and he wrote a book titled *Young Man From Denver*, about his father-newspaperman, author and screenwriter Gene Fowler, who was Murray's favorite writer.

In late 1915, my grandfather was a young police reporter in Denver, Colorado, and he and Gene Fowler, who worked for the *Rocky Mountain News*, got into a poker game on a Saturday night at the Denver Press Club with a group that included a character named Col. Gideon B. McFail, Lee Casey, a columnist from the *News*, and Charlie Carson, a composing room foreman at the *News*. McFail was an "associate" member of the club, but it wasn't known exactly what he did for a living. Most of the time he'd hang around to play cards and politely take the other members' money.

A blizzard was forecast for Denver, so McFail suggested the

game be moved to his home in the Park Hill area of the city, and it was. The blizzard trapped the four men in the house for five days, but instead of stopping the game, they drank all of McFail's whiskey, about two cases worth, burned the furniture and whatever else was combustible to keep warm. By Thursday, the Denver fire department showed up to rescue Carson, who was needed in the stereotype room to help publish the paper.

Both Gene Fowler and my grandfather left Denver for New York City and jobs on the Hearst-owned *Herald Tribune* during the Roaring Twenties. Will Fowler's godfather was Jack Dempsey, and among his friends Will was regarded as the best of raconteurs.

William was the wealthy owner of a company that made macaroni and other kinds of pasta shells. He spent much of his time on the golf course at Riviera Country Club and played every year in the pro-am of the L.A. Open.

Bob was the type of hustler who, on a putt outside the leather, would say "that's good" to his partner, but then on the last hole, with the money on the line, would make the poor sucker putt the two-footer. Or he would wager double or nothing at the 18th hole, which at Riviera was like stealing money because No. 18 is one of the world's famously tough holes. It's a feat just to get a drive up the hill that faces the tee box, and then onto the narrow fairway.

In 1982, William teed off on the first hole in the L.A. Open's pro-am, splitting the fairway with a nice drive. The gallery that surrounded the tee box cheered, and someone yelled, "He's played this course before!"

William was giving Page a lesson on the long pitch shot, trying hard not to put a divot in the carpet. Page was known as Dynamite Don, a television columnist in L.A. who worked at the *Herald-Examiner* and later at the *Times*. It wasn't clear why he was called Dynamite. He had a laid-back disposition and had a reputation, at least at the *Times*, for not working too hard. There was nothing explosive about his personality except that Page enjoyed getting lit up in the bars at Ricky's Valley Inn in Sherman

Oaks and the Pump Room in Studio City, where he spent more of his time than in a newspaper office.

The person missing from this group was Archie Altounian, another Riviera regular who played with Dean Martin. Martin once gave Altounian a new golf bag that had on it the engraved inscription, "Archie the Armenian Hustler." Murray would get a call from Archie before the first round of a major golf tournament, such as the U.S. Open or the Masters. They had a regular bet where Altounian could pick any five golfers he wanted and Murray would take the field.

At stake was a lunch and Jim usually won. I started making the same bet with Murray and the one time I didn't have to buy at Love's was when Greg Norman won the British Open in 1986.

Murray was comfortable around these rogues because when he was a boy in Hartford during the Depression, characters of the same type were always around his grandfather's house. He said one of his uncles warmed up a pair of dice each morning on the stove along with his breakfast eggs.

William handed me the 8-iron and asked me to give his lesson a try. I swung the club, and pretended the shot sailed through Gerry's picture window, then handed the club back. "Yep," William said, "he can get the club on the ball."

We left for the Coliseum. Kickoff was one o'clock but Jim had to be there early to appear on a television show hosted by Pat Sajak, a local TV weatherman who would go on to emcee the immensely popular game show *Wheel of Fortune.*

On the Santa Monica freeway, as "My Fair Lady" played on the tape deck, Jim said, "the Genius called me last night." The Genius was Al Davis, the managing partner of the Raiders. Murray kiddingly called him the Genius because of Davis' ability to put a playoff-caliber football team on the field season after season. Jim liked to say that Al "could spot a football player from the back of a moving train."

"He wanted to know what I thought of his moving the Raiders

to Los Angeles," Jim said. It was ironic that the Rams were playing the Raiders that day. Here they were about to start their last season in L.A. before moving south to Anaheim. They would still be called the Los Angeles Rams, but Orange County was a distance not only in miles but in culture from Brentwood, Bel-Air and the Westside. The majority of the team's season ticket holders lived west of Doheny Drive, and Jim predicted that as time went on, fewer people would drive the 35 miles to see a game. Hollywood would have to look for a new team.

The Rams' move was put in motion on July 13, 1972, when Robert Irsay purchased the club from the estate of Dan Reeves, the team's benevolent owner who had died in April of the previous year. Irsay then transferred ownership to Carroll Rosenbloom, who owned the Baltimore Colts. The two swapped teams and when Rosenbloom and his wife Georgia moved West, Carroll announced that he wanted to make the Rams' golden horns as famous an insignia as the pinstripes of the New York Yankees.

As the Rosenblooms took command, the team was in a rebuilding period under Coach Tommy Prothro. Reeves had hired the former UCLA coach in 1971 after he fired George Allen, who would become the coach of the Washington Redskins.

Instead of developing young talent, Allen preferred experienced veterans, some of whom were at the end of their careers. He was once caught trading draft choices he didn't have for older players. At Washington, Allen raided the Rams defense with a trade that left Prothro with draft choices, but not much else.

But Prothro's keen sense for drafting, picking such future stars as Jack Youngblood, Larry Brooks, Isaiah Robertson, Cullen Bryant, Dave Elmendorf and Lawrence McCutcheon, would help make the team a winner as time went on. Prothro had great success at UCLA and Oregon State, coaching both the Bruins and the Beavers to Rose Bowl appearances. Like his mentor Red Sanders, he was a Southerner from Memphis, Tennessee, and he had a slow-talking, folksy demeanor. When he was trying to decide between taking defensive tackle Larry Brooks and another player in the 14th round of the 1972 draft, Tommy finally said, "Aw, let's take the big turd from Virginia State."

On game day, Prothro showed up on the sidelines wearing a suit, tie, and a hat and carried a briefcase, which contained his lunch. He was a chain-smoker and he looked more like an accountant than a football coach. Unlike his college players, Tommy didn't think professionals needed to be baby-sat, but it was the wrong assessment of this Rams squad. Instead of a peanut butter and jelly sandwich and a can of Coca-Cola in the briefcase, Prothro should have packed a disciplinarian's whip.

After an embarrassing loss to the Denver Broncos at the Coliseum, Prothro gathered his team at a closed-door meeting in the locker room. Wide receiver Jack Snow was late getting off the field because he had stopped to talk with two of the Bronco players. Prothro stuck his head out the door and yelled, "Snow, let's go!" But Jack ignored his coach and went on talking. Prothro shouted again, "Snow!" and he slowly walked to the door and went inside.

One Los Angeles football writer, the *Times'* Bob Oates, who was a loyalist of George Allen, criticized Prothro. Tommy came to the Rams without prior NFL experience. Oates' commentaries jabbed at Prothro's practice-field drills, calling them too collegiate for the pro game. Oates also dug at the plays Prothro called. Tommy's briefcase not only contained his lunch, it also held a variety of gimmicks including a third-down quick kick, a surprise play he sometimes used at UCLA.

Tommy was once asked what he thought of Oates, who rarely went to the Rams' practices or the after-game dressing room, and, in his Tennessee drawl, said, "I never met the man but I sure would like to coach against him."

In Prothro's first season, the Rams were 8-5-1 and finished in second place in the NFC West. But in 1972, they fell to 6-7-1. Rosenbloom didn't have the patience to wait for the young prospects, and he felt their development should be in the hands of a more experienced NFL coach. Also, it was rumored that he was losing thousands of dollars each Sunday betting on his team, so he fired Prothro and hired Chuck Knox, an offensive assistant with the Detroit Lions and a conservative grinder.

Rosenbloom wanted a winner because he planned to remodel the Coliseum, which had been built in the 1920s and expanded to its present form for the 1932 Summer Olympics. Carroll envisioned entertaining wealthy corporate and celebrity season ticket holders in luxury boxes that would encircle the field. He knew they wouldn't buy these seats to watch a 6-7-1 club.

Murray was on cordial terms with the Rosenblooms until one Sunday in 1976 when an agitated Carroll stopped Jim in the Coliseum press box. He was upset about two stories that had appeared in the *Times'* sport section. One article was on Snow, the All-American from Notre Dame who had recently been cut from the roster. Snow was rated third on the club's depth chart at wide receiver, behind Harold Jackson and Ron Jessie. He was angry with Rosenbloom and accused him of breaking a promise that the Rams would trade Snow if he didn't make the team.

The second article was on quarterback James Harris. In the story, Harris accused the press of being racially prejudiced against him, the first black quarterback to play long-term in the NFL. He was unhappy that he wasn't the recipient of the large amounts of publicity that the league's white quarterbacks, including Fran Tarkenton, Terry Bradshaw and Roger Staubach, were getting even though Harris' passing statistics were comparable.

Rosenbloom asked Murray what he thought of the stories, and also of the writer, Skip Bayless, a newcomer at the paper whose writing Bill Shirley wanted to showcase. Jim said he couldn't comment on the stories or give an opinion of a colleague in public. Rosenbloom was furious, shouting, "Colleague, colleague!" He turned and stormed away and didn't speak to Murray for some time. "It was a frosty six months," Jim recalled.

Rosenbloom's plan to refurbish the old stadium ran into the same red tape and bureaucratic entanglements from the Coliseum Commission, the stadium's governing board of city, county and state officials, that Jack Kent Cooke tangled with in the mid-1960s when he desired a fitting arena for the Lakers and his NHL expansion hockey team, the Kings. Cooke was a Canadian and hockey was his first love. He wanted his teams to play in a better area of the city and in something more attractive than the cosmetically drab Sports Arena. But City Hall wasn't about to do for Cooke what it had done for Walter O'Malley, which was give him the land and money to construct his arena. When O'Malley moved the Dodgers from Brooklyn, the politicians awarded him land in the Chavez Ravine area near downtown L.A. and the financial support to build Dodger Stadium. There would be no more Chavez Ravines for the owners of L.A.'s sports franchises. In the end, Cooke thumbed his nose at the politicians and took his teams to suburban Inglewood, where he built his "Fabulous Forum."

But Rosenbloom found a way when the city of Anaheim entered the Rams' picture. It made Carroll a sweet offer that included an expanded Anaheim Stadium, with luxury suites, an area next door for a new practice facility and land for his own private and commercial development. With an aging stadium, sagging attendance (USC football outdrew the Rams by an average of 25,000 a game), and politicians who elbowed and postured, at times with their own agendas, Rosenbloom couldn't refuse the invitation, and he announced that the Rams would be in Orange County by the start of the 1980 season.

But, tragically, he never saw Opening Day. Rosenbloom drowned on April 2, 1979, as he swam in the ocean near his vacation home at Golden Beach, Florida. A rumor lingered that the 72-year-old, who reportedly was an excellent swimmer and had gone into this part of the Atlantic many times, might have been murdered, that an eerie, dark figure was seen in the surf. Police and FBI investigations, though, found no evidence of a crime.

Control of the Rams fell into the hands of Georgia Rosenbloom, who had no tenure in the day-to-day business of an NFL franchise. Her knowledge of football was also lacking. On a plane ride home from a game, she turned to a Rams beat writer who was sitting in the seat behind her and her husband and said that she could make the opposing team's field goal kicker miss by putting a hex on him.

An angry Rosenbloom told her to "shut up," then turned to the writer, "You're not going to print that?"

It was presumed by team officials and the media that Steve Rosenbloom, the club's vice president who had worked at his father's side for many years, would take the helm, but in an ugly family spat that boiled in the sports pages, Georgia fired her stepson.

I parked just a few steps from the Coliseum press box and we walked around to the open end of the stadium where the set of Sajak's show had been built, on the steps below the Olympic torch. It overlooked the field and I could see Georgia on the sideline as she watched her team warm up. Her blonde hair and summer dress blew in the warm September wind.

Jim was one of three guests to appear on Sajak's show, which was a weekend-on-the-town feature program. The topic of their conversation was free agency and the emerging atmosphere of athletes who got richer and talked less to the press. Sajak asked Jim his view of the situation and Murray said that professional sports teams owed it to the media, especially to newspapers, to have players give their time because it was in both the team's and the player's best interests.

"You've got guys with holes in their shoes promoting baseball players who are making hundreds of thousands of dollars," Murray said. Jim blamed television partly for the problem, citing the multimillion-dollar contracts that the TV networks had signed with baseball, the NFL and the NBA. In 1980, the NFL would negotiate a record contract with CBS for $12 million to televise its games. The money gave teams the cash to sign star players while the networks took control of scheduling. For example, the start times of baseball's playoffs and World Series were now at the discretion of TV programming executives and beer company sponsors.

Jim pointed out that when Walter O'Malley was seriously considering the Dodgers' move out of Brooklyn, one of the first things he wanted to know was how many newspapers there were in L.A. O'Malley knew he would need as much coverage as he could get for the transition to work.

Murray was as relaxed on television as he was talking with someone on a street corner. Two years after Jim came to the *Times*, he was interviewed by Steve Bailey on radio station KMPC, which broadcast the Rams' games in Los Angeles. The Rams in the early 1960s were one of the worst teams in the NFL.

Coached by Bob Waterfield, and then by Harland Svare, they had bumbled their way to just 5 wins in two seasons (1961 and 1962). One of the few noteworthy items about the team was who would play quarterback, Zeke Bratkowski or Frank Ryan. In 1962, the controversy roiled around Bratkowski and Roman Gabriel.

Bailey smartly introduced Murray, saying, "Ladies and gentlemen, we have *L.A. Times* sports columnist and funnyman Jim Murray as our halftime guest. Say something funny, Jim." And, on the air, Murray coolly said, "The Rams."

After Sajak signed off, we rode up in the press box elevator with a group of people that included composer Henry Mancini, and then watched the game from the *Times'* seats. The skyline of downtown Los Angeles stood crystal-clear against the San Gabriels. In the hills, the Hollywood sign glistened like a white emblem, an enticing welcome mat to the visitors from Oakland. The Raiders, the future tenants of the Coliseum, beat the outbound Rams, 24-17, behind a fourth-quarter rally led by the pinpoint passing of quarterback Ken Stabler.

After the game, Murray went to the Raiders locker room. Al Davis shook his hand, put his arm around his shoulder, and gave him a big welcome, saying what a great team the Rams were and how lucky the Raiders were to win the game. Like the Dodgers' O'Malley two decades before him, Davis knew he would need the media in his corner when he would make his controversial move south in 1982.

106

Glad-handing L.A.'s biggest media star was Al's overture. Even some of the Raiders players seemed to be in on the audition. Linebacker Phil Villapiano gushed about the Coliseum's "great field," and what a pleasure it was to play on it.

Stabler, on the other hand, leaned against a wall still dressed in most of his uniform, and he sipped a can of beer. His nickel-gray hair was soaked with sweat and he talked about some time he had spent on the beaches of Alabama, before the exhibition season. Stabler's short-to-medium passes never fit well with Davis' beloved vertical scheme, which called for quick, deep strikes down the field from a strong-armed quarterback such as Daryl Lamonica or Jay Schroeder. Even though he was the Raiders' all-time leader in passing yards and touchdowns, Stabler, known as the Snake, fell out of favor with Davis and he was traded after the 1979 season to the Houston Oilers, leaving his legacy in Oakland.

Actor James Garner, a big Raiders fan and friend of the team's legendary place kicker, George Blanda, stood next to Stabler and when he saw Murray, his face beamed. "Hey, Jimmy, how are you, it's nice to see you again." Garner's welcome was genuine, one Riviera golfer to another. There wasn't a hint of glad-handing, just a friendly handshake.

****

In September, Murray wrote columns on Kent Tekulve, the Pirates' submarine-style relief pitcher; Olympic swimmer Mark Spitz; the Dodgers' third baseman, Ron Cey; L.A.'s grand master of tennis, Jack Kramer; USC tailback Charles White; Edward Bennett Williams, the Washington lawyer who owned the Baltimore Orioles; boxing promoter Eileen Eaton; and the Raiders' stellar punter, Ray Guy. This collection of subjects reflected the diversity of sports in the month—the 30-day period is a veritable feast for a sports fan.

Of Tekulve, Jim said, *"The first gander you get at Kent Tekulve, the Pittsburgh Pirates pitcher, you gather he wasn't born, he was drawn by Norman Rockwell. He is Ichabod Crane in cleats. If you put a stamp on him you could mail him anywhere. He's somewhere between 6½ and 7½ feet tall and somewhere between 100 and 160 pounds. When he goes swimming, he looks like an eel with glasses on. He could hide behind a rake."*

Baseball's pennant races had come to the wire, with the play-offs and World Series waiting in the wings. The college and pro football seasons were under way; soccer and tennis matches, including the U.S. Open, were plentiful; and the doors of the fall camps for NHL and NBA had opened. Summer vacation was over for the sports department, and coverage of all these events, especially the Angels' bid to win the American League's West Division, was at a premium.

In Los Angeles, the Angels were the hot story and would continue to be until they either won or were eliminated. Next came the Rams, followed by USC and UCLA football. The Dodgers had moved up into third place in the National League West but were out of the pennant race, so their game stories were played on an inside page of the section. With so many teams, it was tricky for a makeup editor to decide what game should go where on the front page. There were a few guide points. Bill Shirley's recommendations were always taken. A great photo might be influential; an upset could have an effect. But what didn't help was when an editor from another department who was either a huge sports fan or had a favorite team, would poke his head into Shirley's office and say, "Hey, the Bruins have a big one on Saturday, how many people are we sending out to the game?" and hope his comment might somehow sway Bill to play UCLA's football game above USC's.

The best example of this problem occurred on Saturday night, September 9 of 1972. USC was to play Arkansas on the road in Little Rock. It was the first game for both teams, and the Razorbacks, who were ranked No. 4 in preseason polls, had national championship aspirations. UCLA was at home against Nebraska, the two-time defending national champion. The consensus before both kickoffs

108

was that USC-Arkansas would be a close contest and the Cornhuskers would handily beat the Bruins. But, the Trojans, who would go on to win the national championship that season, routed the Razorbacks, 31-10. Quarterback Mike Rae passed for 269 yards, completing 18 of 24 passes. And the Bruins, with Mark Harmon at the controls of the offense's wishbone formation and the defense holding fast against the Cornhuskers' quarterback David Humm, stunned Nebraska, 20-17, on Efren Herrera's game-winning 30-yard field goal.

But earlier in the evening, a bulletin from Munich, Germany, sent everything into a tizzy. The United States was upset, 51-50, by the Soviet Union in basketball—the first time America lost a basketball game in Olympic history. The game ended in controversy because the referees put time back on the clock three times after Hank Iba's squad—which included Jim Brewer, Tom McMillen, Ed Ratleff and Doug Collins, all future NBA players—thought it had won in regulation. The extra seconds gave the Soviets' star player, a blond-haired giant named Alexander Belov, enough time to take a long pass and muscle in to score the winning basket.

Chuck Garrity, the news editor that night, suddenly had three major stories and little time to decide how they should be played. The phones started to ring with callers who had watched the basketball game on TV. Their reaction ranged from disbelief to outrage, and the significance of the loss, the first for the U.S. in 63 games, helped push the basketball game above USC's win and UCLA's upset. Garrity played Murray's column at the top of the page. Jim wrote on the arrogant behavior and bad manners displayed by the U.S. track and field team in Munich. The column was followed by the basketball game story, written by Dwight Chapin.

On Monday morning, two assistant managing editors complained to Shirley, who had been in Little Rock to cover USC and Arkansas, about the layout of the Sunday sports section. Leonard Riblett was a UCLA fan, the other editor, Ted Weegar, was a Trojan diehard. The editors in sports had a name for these people—they were called "honks." Art Wild, the night liaison

109

between the *Times'* downtown office and its Orange County facility, was a Stanford honk.

Both Riblett and Weegar thought their teams' football games were underplayed and it was a good example of why newsside editors shouldn't meddle in sports section decision making. Over time, it was proven that Garrity had made the right call because the Americans' loss to the Soviets would be written and talked about for years.

The worst example of newsside intrusion came when managing editor Frank Haven one day decided that the NBA box scores took up too much space, and he ordered them cut from the paper. The next morning angry readers flooded the *Times'* telephone switchboard with protests. There were so many calls that Avrum Dansky, who had come in on his day off to update his stats, got tired of answering the phone and transferred the calls to Haven's office. Frank lumbered down to the sports department and saw only Dansky at the copy desk. He shouted, "Who's sending those calls to my phone?" But Dansky didn't answer. He kept his head down and did his work. The next day the box scores were back in the paper.

I told Murray these stories as we drove to have lunch with swimmer Mark Spitz at a small cafe in Brentwood Village. Spitz's record seven gold medals at Munich had made him a star of the Games. He had comfortably retired from competition to work in the lucrative business of building condominiums with his father-in-law, Herm Weiner, on L.A.'s desirable Westside. He also dabbled in racing sailboats and sports cars. Jim asked him why he didn't make a play for Hollywood, as swimmers Buster Crabbe and Johnny Weissmuller did after their medal-winning Olympic performances. Crabbe starred as space voyager Buck Rodgers in the 1930s and Weissmuller swung from the trees in five *Tarzan* films.

Spitz said, "In this life there are players and there are conductors. I felt more comfortable as a conductor. I never intended to become a movie star.

"Oh, I had seen Joe Namath shave on television and that sort of thing, and it occurred to me I could pick up some fast money.

But I enjoyed running a business, rather than having a business run me."

Murray had been at the Munich Games, too, and was in the city on the morning of September 5, 1972, when eight Palestinian terrorists sneaked into the Olympic Village and took hostage eleven Israeli athletes. Jim was awakened by a phone call from Joe Alex Morris, the *Times'* correspondent in Bonn. Murray answered the phone in a groggy voice and heard Morris say, "Do you need any help with that situation down there?" Jim asked, "What situation?" Morris told him what had happened and updated him on what he knew. Murray hung up the phone and quickly got dressed.

He hurried down to the lobby to get a cab and ran into Howard Cosell and Jim McKay. The three agreed to share a ride to the Olympic Village. McKay was taking a customary morning swim in the hotel's pool when he heard the news. He was in such a hurry to change his clothes that he forgot to take off his wet swim trunks. He just pulled his pants over them. On the way, Cosell plotted how he would get past the German security guards and into the Village.

For the Olympics, the Munich police wore powder-blue uniforms that made them look less officious and also less conspicuous at the venues. Security's soft image made Cosell think it would be easy to talk his way in. But Murray cautioned him, saying, "Don't kid yourself, Howard, these are the sons of the Gestapo."

Murray, McKay and Cosell were among the first newsmen to arrive at the Olympic Village. The *Times'* Dwight Chapin had been sent out of the city on an assignment by sports features editor Jack Quigg, and he didn't learn of the crisis until he returned later that night.

Cosell did manage to get in and ABC broadcast his reports, which were the first from any newsman inside the Village. Two athletes had been killed in their residences. The horrific drama concluded at the Munich airport where the other nine died after a botched rescue attempt by German police sharpshooters. That night, Murray wrote a column that ran on the front page of the *Times'* main news section. The lead read, *"I stood on a rooftop balcony on the Connollystrasse in the Olympic Village Tuesday and witnessed an Olympic event Baron de Coubertin never dreamed of and the purpose of which is as arcane to me as the discus, the team foil, the hammer, individual epee or Greco-Roman wrestling.*

"An Arab rifle team, arriving late, scorned the small-bore rifle, three positions, the free pistol (silhouette) and introduced a new event to the Olympic program—murder."

This was one of just two columns of Jim's that didn't run in the sports section. The other was a tribute to Ben Hogan when the golf legend died in 1997.

Chapter Seven

CHERUBS, A 7-IRON AND AN MVP

"The summer night is like a perfection of thought."
—Wallace Stevens

Gene Autry stood at the door of the main entrance to Anaheim Stadium. He wore a beautifully tailored brown leather and suede jacket, tan slacks and boots. In his hand was a handsome white cowboy hat. Autry held the door open for Jim Murray, who had come to the ballpark along with the sellout crowd to see if Autry's Angels could win their first championship. The Angels were in first place in the American League's West and a win on that night, September 27, 1979, would give Gene the title he had dreamed of since he sat on a Schwinn bicycle in 1961 and rode with his expansion players to their first spring workout in Palm Springs.

It's extraordinary for an owner of a sports team to wait on a sportswriter. Most stayed away from the press box. Lakers owner Jerry Buss would give one interview a year. But Murray wasn't any sportswriter. When Rod Carew had decided to boycott the media, especially the Angel beat writers, Murray went to the ballpark and sat at the end of the dugout with the future Hall of Fame hitter to see what his problem was. When one of the writers saw Carew with Murray, he said, "Hey, how come he'll talk to him but not to us?" The fellow obviously didn't understand that it was because it was Jim Murray.

Also, Autry and Murray had an unusual bond—they both had suffered detached retinas. Like Murray, Autry had been a patient of Dr. Charles Scheppens, the Boston eye specialist. When Jim's retina detached, he was told after the surgery that 90 percent of all reattached retinas stay up. When he heard that Autry's surgery had been a success and that Gene could see, it gave Murray hope until he remembered the story of Lefty Gomez, the New York Yankees' exceptional left-hand pitcher from the 1930s. Gomez had a dream of a fastball and he won 21 games in 1931. He would help New York win five pennants and five World Series in that decade.

Lefty eventually developed arm trouble, but doctors told him that only 10 percent of players with his problem didn't come back to pitch. Gomez was relieved to hear the news until a stab of fear went through him when he realized that he could be in that 10 percent that never stepped onto a big league mound again. Gomez returned to pitch, but Murray was among the 10 percent of retina patients who lost their sight.

Murray and Autry rode the elevator to the press box and when the two parted, Gene went to watch the game with Richard Nixon, who was a frequent guest at the ballpark that summer. Nixon lived in San Clemente, on the beach in Casa de Pacifica, the estate that had been the Western White House when he was president. He was an avid baseball fan and had adopted the Angels as his team.

The 1979 Angels were the franchise's best since the 1962 club that was the talk of the American League when it challenged the New York Yankees for the pennant. The 1979 team had six All-Stars—Don Baylor, Rod Carew, pitcher Mark Clear, catcher Brian Downing, second baseman Bobby Grich and pitcher Nolan Ryan. Carew, the seven-time AL batting champion, had come to Anaheim from the Minnesota Twins, as did outfielder Dan Ford.

Known as Disco Dan, Ford was an effective addition to the lineup, hitting .290, with 101 runs batted-in and 100 runs scored.

Murray settled into a seat in the press box as Frank Tanana took the mound against George Brett and the Kansas City Royals.

Tanana, a left-hander out of Detroit, had recorded 200 strike-outs for three straight seasons. His fastball had been nearly as good as Ryan's, but where Ryan took care of himself physically, Tanana had a reputation for playing hard off the field. When Dick Williams managed the team, he took Frank aside one day and asked him, "Why do most of the bartenders in Orange County know you?"

After winning 18 games in 1978, Tanana's record dipped to 7-5 in 1979, mostly because of a sore arm. Despite his poor season, Jim Fregosi put the ball and the team's destiny into his glove, and Tanana delivered. He pitched a five-hitter and beat the Royals, 4-1. While the team celebrated on the field, the Angel's PR staff escorted the press corps to the Angels clubhouse. Murray and I couldn't keep up and we missed the first elevator. But we caught the next one and when we got off I could see the writers running down a long ramp to the clubhouse door. As television reporters with their cameramen in tow hurried past us, I took Murray by the arm and coaxed him to move faster. John Strege of the *Orange County Register* caught up with us, and just as we got to the door, it started to close. Strege and I yelled, "Hey, wait, open the door." Fortunately, a clubhouse attendant heard us and we got in.

The Secret Service had ordered the door shut because Autry had brought Nixon in to see the team. Jim stood off to the side of the room where plastic sheets covered the lockers to protect the players' clothes. Champagne was being sprayed everywhere. Nixon was in the middle, and the players drenched him with the bubbly and cans of beer. The press surrounded him and he was delighted by the attention. Nixon offered Autry and his players congratulations and then took questions about the team and its chances in its upcoming playoff series with the Baltimore Orioles.

It seemed that the writers wanted to talk to the former president more than the Angel players.

Autry went over to Fregosi who tried to catch his breath from the excitement. Fregosi had done as a manager what he couldn't do as an All-Star shortstop in Los Angeles and Anaheim, which was win a pennant for Autry, his baseball surrogate father. In 1962, the Angels were in first place on July 4 after sweeping a holiday doubleheader from the Washington Senators. "Heaven Can Wait! Angels in 1st on 4th," read the headline in the *Times* sports section.

But the Angels were there only for one day. They fell behind the Yankees in August and were later buried by New York in a crucial three-game series at Yankee Stadium that cinched a bittersweet third-place finish.

The Angels had to fight the American League on one front and the Dodgers on another. They had Fregosi, but they needed more players like him to compete with the Yankees and also draw better attendance. As tenants of the Dodgers for four seasons, they played before medium to sparse crowds. Fregosi said, "The Dodgers had sellouts every night. We had family and friends."

At a dinner for the Angels and Dodgers sponsored by the local chapter of the Baseball Writers of America, Maury Wills was honored for breaking Ty Cobb's single-season record for stolen bases. After Wills accepted his award, Fred Haney, the Angels general manager, said, "Congratulations, Maury, and we're going to get one like you real soon."

The Angels desperately needed a superstar and Autry thought he had one when the team signed third baseman Rick Reichardt off the campus of the University of Wisconsin. Reichardt was a multi-sport athlete for the Badgers, and, as a member of the football team, had played in the 1963 Rose Bowl against USC. Some in the Angels organization saw Reichardt as the next Mickey Mantle. He was a strapping 6-foot-3 and weighed 212 pounds. He could hit, hit with power, run and throw, and he was rushed into the major league team's lineup with a $200,000 bonus, the largest in baseball history.

At the same time, the Dodgers signed Willie Crawford, a young eighteen-year-old African-American outfielder from Fremont High School in Los Angeles.

The Dodgers, a pennant-winning-caliber team, had the luxury to slowly bring Crawford along, letting him develop into a better-than-average ballplayer who would play in L.A. for eleven seasons.

But Reichardt, hampered by injuries and a lack of seasoning, never became what the Angels dreamed. His best year for home runs was 1968 when he hit 21.

After just nine games of the 1970 season, a stretch in which he hit .167, the Angels traded him to the Senators. The fact was that the Angels could have signed Crawford in 1963, but they already had Leon Wagner, a black outfielder who had a contentious relationship with the front office. Wagner had 37 home runs and 107 RBIs in his All-Star season of 1962, but he bickered with Haney over his salary, and their relationship deteriorated when Wagner called the Angel executive "Khrushchev."

Starving for a superstar, preferably a white one, the Angels chose Reichardt instead of Crawford.

With their small-crowd appeal (the paid attendance for the Angels' last game in Los Angeles was 945) and existing in the shadow of the success of the Dodgers, Autry moved the team to Anaheim in 1965 as the California Angels.

Fregosi was traded to the New York Mets in 1971 for four players including pitchers Nolan Ryan and Lee Stanton, a transaction that was a steal for California. But though the Angels had Ryan, a future Hall of Famer, the losing seasons continued from 1971 to 1977. In 1978, Autry brought Fregosi home from Pittsburgh, where he had been reserve infielder. "When you get to my age [37], there are no routine ground balls," Fregosi said at the time.

He replaced Dave Garcia, and now at the helm of a team with a purpose, he had accomplished what he was hired to do. The banner headline in the *Times* the next morning read, "Autry Finally Gets Another Champion."

117

A day later, Murray wrote on Tanana. *"The other night, Frank Tanana kept serving up unpleasant surprises to the Kansas City Royals. It was like opening packages all night for the Royals and getting hit in the eye with a rubber snake. Frank Tanana's fast ball was considered just faster than a glacier. It needed tugboats. You didn't catch it, you docked it. Every pitch was like finding a man in your closet, or a stranger in a dark alley, or your car stolen.*
He didn't pitch the ball up there, he smuggled it."

It had been an historic night. The paths of Murray and Richard Nixon had crossed again after 27 years and although Jim didn't speak to him, he raised his eyebrows slightly when I told him what Nixon looked like soaked in champagne. And, the Angels had finally made the playoffs, against feisty Earl Weaver and his high-flying Baltimore Orioles.

****

The first two games of the American League Championship Series were to be played at Memorial Stadium in Baltimore. Murray decided to let baseball rest and, in an interlude, wrote on Anne Meyers, the All-American UCLA basketball player who had led the Bruins to the women's national championship in 1978.

Meyers was in the news because she had signed a contract with the Indiana Pacers, becoming the first woman to join an NBA team. Murray interviewed her at her office in West Hollywood, and afterward we drove out Sunset Boulevard to Pacific Palisades to have lunch with Charles Hathaway at Riviera Country Club. Hathaway was one of the top executives of the Los Angeles Athletic Club, which was affiliated with Riviera.

Our visit put Jim in the mood to talk about Ben Hogan and golf, which was Murray's favorite sport; at least, it was the one he wrote some of his best columns about. Lunch was served in the clubhouse, in a private dining room that overlooked the course's famous 18th hole. Murray had written on both Hogan and Riviera many times, and the articles included a cover story on The Hawk for *Time* in 1949. As part of his salary, the magazine had given Murray a membership at Riviera, but when he went to the *Times*, the paper wouldn't pay his monthly dues. Because of the cost, Jim had it reduced to a half-membership, and he rarely played the course after 1980.

Murray regarded Hogan as the best striker of the golf ball who ever lived.

Hogan was the exception when Jim said you can't become friends with the athletes you cover. Their families socialized in Palm Desert and Jim idolized the man, saying after Hogan's death that Ben was held to a higher standard than the rest of the sports world.

Jim once was standing behind the ropes during a practice round for a tournament when a group of players that included Arnold Palmer came along.

Palmer saw Murray and called, "Come on, Jim, join us." So Murray climbed over the yellow rope and followed Arnie. On one hole, Palmer put his drive down the right side of the fairway and it landed in an area covered with leaves, pine cones and debris that included a soda pop can, and he was left with a difficult second shot. When he got to the ball, Palmer turned to Murray and said, "All right, Smarty, what would your pal Hogan do here?" Jim looked at Arnold and said, "Hogan wouldn't be here."

Jim had some timeless lines about golf and used them regularly in his columns. His favorites included "I'm a big fan of double bogeys"; "Golf is like life, it isn't fair"; and "There are worse jobs than umpiring or digging ditches—putting for a living comes to mind."

In 1983, he was at Rancho Park golf course in West Los Angeles. The L.A. Open had been moved to the public course on Pico Boulevard because Riviera, where the local PGA tournament was usually played, was to be the host that year of the PGA Championship. He stood along the fairway on the 9th hole when George Archer approached. Archer had pushed his drive into the trees, and as he searched for his ball, his playing partner prepared

119

to hit from where his drive had landed in the middle of the fairway. I started to walk over to watch the second shot, an easy 7-iron to the green, about 150 yards away, when Archer located his ball and then tried to figure out how to get out of the mess he was in. His route back to the fairway and down to the green was obstructed by bushes and tree trunks. Murray asked me, "Where are you going?" I told him I wanted to watch Archer's partner hit his second shot. And Jim said, "Are you kidding? This is the shot."

At Riviera, Murray liked to watch play where the 9th hole, the 10th tee, the 2nd hole and the 18th hole were all in proximity of each other. During the third round of the PGA Championship, he stood on the lower steps of a path that led up to the clubhouse. As he watched Jack Nicklaus tee off on No. 10, he gazed at the vista of sycamore trees and green fairways that was haloed by the morning fog, then turned around and said, "Isn't it magnificent?" I thought he meant Nicklaus, but he said, "Look at that clubhouse, isn't it magnificent?" The gorgeous Spanish-style structure on the bluff above the course was magnificent, a breathtaking sight, like a castle on a hill.

During the PGA, Nicklaus, who never won a tournament at Riviera, said that it was a good course, "but not as great as Murray thinks it is." It galled Jim when someone shot a 63 on Hogan's Alley, named so by the caddies after Hogan won three tournaments in two years there in the late 1940s, especially if the player wasn't well known. Murray smiled with glee when the wind whipped off the Pacific Ocean and coaxed balls into the thick Kikuyu grass and the nearly inescapable barranca. There would be a glint in his eye when the greens dried from the Santa Ana winds and became lightning fast, and scores would soar.

During a practice round for the PGA, Jim bumped into Gary Player who was about to hit his ball at the 18th tee. Murray asked the South African great what score would be good enough to win. Player thought for a few seconds, then teed up his ball and drove it straight up the hill, and safely to the middle of the fairway.

He turned back to Murray and said, "Ten under!" Player's

prediction was on the mark. Hal Sutton won with a 10-under score of 274.

After the first round of the tournament, Murray wrote a column that said Nicklaus' reign as golf's best player was over. "*I put on the dark glasses, the black visor and slunk on the edges of the gallery Thursday as the old champion went out for one more main event, another chapter in the legend of the greatest player ever to play the game. I wasn't there when Dempsey couldn't find Tunney, but I was there when Riviera was helpless, tied to the ropes, unable to defend itself and nobodies were copping Sundays on it, shooting 65s and 66s and landing round houses. And Nicklaus couldn't lay a glove on it.*

I was there when he kept missing KO punches and let it jab him to death and add a jeer by double-bogeying him on the last hole. Is this Dempsey climbing in the ring in Chicago, Louis trying to call on old remembered skills one more time, Tilden thinking he can fool one more serve, Cousy trying to get the ball past one more back court hot shot with the same old behind-the-back magic?

"Nicklaus hasn't won a major since 1980. He hasn't won a tournament of any kind in over a year. The putts are longer, the traps are deeper. Dempsey could tell him the feeling. So could Budge, Thorpe, Grange, Ruth, Cousy.

"Riviera could be Tunney. It could be Lefty Grove to Ruth. Oscar Robertson to Cousy. The Kid's last fight, the last opponent. I'm sorry I saw it."

Jack finished second and had a chance to send the tournament into a playoff on the 72nd hole but missed a putt for birdie that left him one stroke behind Sutton. After the tournament, the letters and calls poured into the sports department, most of them from Nicklaus fans who criticized Murray for the column. But it turned out Jim's point was accurate. Although Nicklaus won the Memorial Tournament in 1984 and a record sixth Masters in 1986 at age 46, his earnings declined from 10th in 1983, to 15th in 1984, to 43rd in 1985, then they took a dramatic drop to 127th in 1987 and fell even farther to 177th in 1988.

****

I was scheduled to work my regular desk shift in the office during Games 1 and 2 of the Angels-Orioles playoffs. When I walked into the sports department on the afternoon of October 3, Marilyn White called me over to her desk. She asked, "Has Bill said anything to you?" I said, "No. About what?" She said, "You're going to the World Series with Murray." I was knocked off my feet and I floated around the office the rest of the night. I couldn't believe it. I was going to the World Series. I had sat in the stands at Dodger Stadium for Game 2 of the Dodgers-Yankees Series in 1978, when Bob Welch dramatically struck out Reggie Jackson in the ninth inning to preserve a Dodgers win. After the Angels won their division, I really pulled for them to get into the Series because then Murray would be assigned to cover the games in Anaheim. Now, it didn't matter who got in.

The best-of-five game series opened in Baltimore with Nolan Ryan pitching against Jim Palmer, a matchup of two future Hall of Famers. The Orioles had a well-balanced team. It played good defense, hit with fair power and had depth on the bench. Also, Earl Weaver had a tremendous pitching staff at his disposal, a starting rotation that included Palmer, Mike Flanagan, a winner of 23 games, Scott McGregor and Dennis Martinez. In the bullpen were Tippy Martinez and Don Stanhouse, who had appeared in 52 games and saved 21 of them. The Orioles played 159 games in 1979 and, remarkably, won 102.

Game 1 went into the 10th inning tied, 3-3, and in the bottom half Weaver sent John Lowenstein up to pinch-hit with two runners on base against reliever John Montague. The left-handed hitting outfielder proceeded to hit an opposite-field three-run home run, down the left-field line that just cleared the fence. Frank Finch had a name for it. It was Lowenstein's third career home run off Montague, who had come to the Angels that season from Seattle.

In a column from Los Angeles, Murray wrote on Don Baylor and why he was a deserving candidate for the league's Most

Valuable Player award. Baylor had led the American League in runs batted-in with 139, and runs scored with 120. He also slugged 36 home runs in a lineup that, at times, was depleted by injuries.

"The fans in Anaheim never seemed to notice Don Baylor was standing alone.

You can't boo outside a hospital window, so Joe Rudi and Bobby Grich were safe. But Baylor was standing up there highly visible at home plate, trying to hit bouncing curveballs because that was all he would get for weeks on end."

"The only way Don Baylor would not have qualified for MVP is in the cut of his uniform. Oh, it fits all right, it's a nice color, red and black, and it's neatly laundered, but only one player wearing the uniform of an expansion team—Jeff Burroughs in 1974—ever won the MVP. If your team wins a championship, and you win the RBI title, get a place ready in your trophy case.

In the past 25 years, every batter who has led the RBI field and driven in more than 130 runs has won the MVP title. And Baylor has 139 runs driven in."

The Angels lost Game 2, 9-8, and faced elimination in Game 3 at Anaheim, but they rallied in the ninth inning for a 4-3 win. Larry Harlow doubled off Stanhouse to drive in the decisive run. Baylor hit a home run and reliever Don Aase got the win. That night Murray called to say he wanted to go to Game 4, which was the next day, Saturday, October 6. Jim planned to try something he hadn't attempted since his return to work, which was write on deadline in the press box. His plan was to stay for the whole game, have me go to the clubhouse for quotes, then he would dictate the column into his tape recorder and play it back over the phone to a transcription typist at the paper.

The Angels started Chris Knapp against the Orioles' stylish left-hander Scott McGregor. McGregor, 25, was a star on the rise in the American League. He started 23 games in 1979 and won 13. In 1980, he would be a 20-game winner. The Orioles had acquired him from the Yankees in a ten-player trade in 1976. He had great control, threw a sharp-breaking curveball at several speeds and had a stealthy pickoff move to first base. Knapp, on the other hand, had suffered a ruptured disc in his back earlier in the season at Yankee Stadium when, on a rainy day in the Bronx, he slipped on the wet mound. The Orioles got to him in the third inning for two runs. Then they scored five more in the seventh off David Frost, who had been a starter throughout the season. Fregosi used every pitcher available, but Pat Kelly drove in three runs with a home run and a single, and McGregor baffled the California batters. He allowed just six hits and pitched a complete game for an 8-0 win, and the American League pennant belonged to Baltimore.

As I hurried to the clubhouse, the sweat trickled off my forehead and the excitement made my hands damp. I got quotes from McGregor and third baseman Doug DeCinces, who had struggled that season in his attempt to replace an institution in Baltimore, the incomparable Brooks Robinson. But DeCinces had made a Robinson-like play, spectacular, in the fifth inning after the Angels had loaded the bases with one out. He dove for hard smash by Jim Anderson that was headed down the left-field line. Somehow he hooked the bag with his foot, then threw to first for a double play. It killed the Angels' rally and saved McGregor.

The Orioles drank champagne but there was little of the usual celebratory dousing in the Baltimore clubhouse. The players were joyous and happy, but many preferred to sit on folding chairs in front of their lockers. It was easy to talk to them. When I got back to the press box, Murray had nearly finished his column. I gave him the quotes and when he was done I found a pay telephone in the hallway outside the Orioles clubhouse. I dialed the paper and made the connection to the transcription department. But, the wire from Jim's tape recorder came loose, so he had to reconnect it and start again.

Midway through the second attempt, Tim Stoddard, one of the Orioles' pitchers, came out of the locker room with a large boombox radio that blasted music at a high volume. At 6 feet, 7 inches, he looked like a jolly giant with the radio on his shoulder and a bottle of champagne in his hand. He smiled, oblivious to Murray who had become upset with the loud music. "Can you turn it down?" Jim yelled. He put the phone to his ear but it had disconnected again. "Damn it!" I asked Stoddard if he could turn down the volume, and explained what Murray was trying to do. As I redialed the phone, Stoddard walked down the hallway, the sound of music trailing off as he went away. The third attempt was a success, and the column went through.

It was written on Rod Carew and how the great hitter had been denied for the 13th consecutive year a chance to play in the World Series. *"Rod Carew is not the only tragic figure of the sport. Ernie Banks, the blue bird of Lake Michigan, is another great player who never made a Series. The great Walter Johnson got into the Series only in his dotage. Al Kaline barely scrambled into one. So did Ted Williams. Not playing in a World Series for a great hitter is like not making the Met for a great singer, not playing the Old Vic for a great actor. Never making the palace for a vaudevillian. Rod Carew bats .388 the way some people tie their shoelaces. Maybe with even less effort.*

"The loss is the game's. A World Series without Rod Carew in it is like a New Year's Eve party with milk. The Baltimore Orioles are a nice-enough group of athletes but, stacked up against a Rod Carew, they come up as gifted semipros. Only two Hall of Fame ballplayers, the legendary Ty Cobb and Honus Wagner, have won more batting titles than Rod Carew."

As we headed back to Bel-Air, I was disappointed that there would be no World Series in Southern California. It would have been nice to have the home team in the Series. Murray was tired, and expressed his frustration that his attempt to file his column on deadline had turned out more difficult than he had anticipated. "Who was that guy with the music?" he finally asked. "Let's stay away from him."

The Angels had had a good season, they made the playoffs, but the Orioles proved they were the better team. Now they would face the Pittsburgh Pirates, who had swept the Cincinnati Reds in the National League's playoffs. I dropped Jim off and went home to pack for the trip to Baltimore.

OCTOBER

Chapter Eight

BAWLMER AND PITTSBAARRRG

"Good pitching will stop good hitting, and vice-versa."
—Casey Stengel

The United Airlines jet circled over Baltimore National Airport
and I could see Memorial Stadium out the window. The ballpark's
lights were on and workers prepared for the opening game of the
76th World Series. "I think there's a baseball game down there
tomorrow night," the pilot said over the plane's intercom.

Gerry Murray had driven Jim and me to the airport for an
afternoon flight to the East Coast. My cohorts in the sports
department had given me some travel tips. They said dress light,
that it would be warm in Maryland. They called it Indian Summer.
"Stay off North Charles Street, Scheib," George Kiseda warned
with a wry smile. North Charles Street was the center of the
golden age of Baltimore's night life in the 1940s and '50s, but it
had turned into a seedy row of bars and was now the town's red-
light district. "Bring me back some Iron City beer, Scheib," was
Marilyn White's request.

"Have a good flight, fellas," Gerry called as the Skycap checked our bags. Jim bought a paperback mystery at a newsrack in the terminal and he tried to read it with his optical telescope as we sat at a table and drank a Coke.

"Here's to a good World Series," I said. We got to two seats in first class. Mine was a jump seat, smaller than the others in the section, but I didn't mind. The 5½-hour flight was smooth all the way. It was the first time I had flown in first class and I was impressed. Murray, on the other hand, had done it many times and he thought the extra service—hot towels, wine and a steak for dinner—wasn't worth the extra $500.

We landed at 8:30 p.m. Eastern Daylight Time and I got a cab that took us to the Hilton Hotel in downtown Baltimore. It was Major League Baseball's headquarters for the Series, and when we walked into the lobby I recognized a lot of faces. Vin Scully and Sparky Anderson were among those who waited to check in at the busy reservation desk. Murray's room was on the floor above mine, and after we got our keys and unpacked our suitcases, we went down to a restaurant off the lobby for something to eat.

There was a large crowd of people at the bar, so I ordered two light beers while Murray sat on a couch. Out of the crowd came a nattily dressed little man with white hair. He approached Jim and sat down next to him. He took Murray's hand and told him who he was. It was Red Smith, the great sports columnist for the *New York Times*. Murray smiled and asked Smith to join us.

Then Tom Lasorda and Cincinnati Reds manager John McNamara appeared along with Mark Heisler, one of the *L.A. Times*' baseball writers and John Strege of the *Orange County Register*. It was a lively group, with Lasorda and McNamara trying to top each other with one baseball story after another. I wish I had had a camera because there was Smith and Murray, arguably the two greatest sportswriters ever, happily chatting away, side by side at the World Series. Jim tried to buy a round of beers but, first Smith, then Lasorda wouldn't let him.

Finally Murray pleaded, "Please, Red, I want to buy." The scene was a highlight start to the trip.

Tuesday, October 9, 1979—The next morning, my body's clock was on Pacific Time. The clock on the night table said 8:00 a.m., but I wanted more sleep. Then I noticed that something wasn't right. There was no sound of cars or buses' horns or people's voices coming from the street three stories below. No sound of airplanes flying overhead. I thought, *Well, this is Baltimore, it's not as noisy as Los Angeles.* Then I looked out the window and saw that the cars parked in front of the hotel and across the street were covered in white. I thought, *That can't be what I think it is.* But it was. A snowstorm had blown in overnight. "There goes tonight's game," I said out loud. Indian Summer looked more like an early winter. The warmest clothes I had were a suit from Saks Fifth Avenue, a pair of jeans and a windbreaker. I got dressed and called Murray's room. He was already up and had been at work on a column for the next day. The plan was for him to write every day of the Series except on the days we traveled. He asked me to go down to the lobby and buy any of the local newspapers. In Baltimore, that would have been the *Sun*, the *Evening Sun* and the *Washington Post*. We ordered room-service breakfast, and, between bites of scrambled eggs and toast, I read the sports sections out loud. Jim had written his Tuesday column before we left L.A. and it ran in the *Times* that morning.

"On paper, it doesn't look like your vintage World Series. It's a club fight. Ernie 'The Rock' Durando vs. Fancy Pants Requejo. A couple of swarmers. Baltimore vs. Pittsburgh. Color it gray. Paint it dull. Dempsey-Tunney it ain't. One team can't hit, the other can't pitch. Look for it to go the route to a split decision."

Murray had brought a stack of scratch paper with him, the same 8½-inch x 11-inch light brown drawing paper he had written his columns on even before his retina detached. For the Series, he would abandon the tape recorder and write in longhand, making big letters that his cataract-covered eye could just see. It took about four pieces of paper for three or four paragraphs. He wrote most of the Wednesday column and would top it that night at the game, if the weather cooperated. The Associated Press' weather story said it was the earliest snowfall of the century, surprising residents of suburban Washington, D.C., and the storm had dropped a foot of snow in West Virginia. The forecast for the rest of the day called for more snow, then rain and cold, with temperatures to dip to the low 30s.

I called the paper and asked Chuck Garrity if I could buy a raincoat or warm jacket and put it on my expense account. I could hear him yell my request into Bill Shirley's office, and Bill answered, "Only if it's a forty-two regular," meaning I would have to give it to him when I got back to L.A.

We went to the Series' hospitality room to get our credentials, a package that included identification, tickets, media guides and season statistics for both the Pirates and the Orioles, a scorebook, pens, a briefcase to carry it all, and most important, the official World Series pin. It was gold with the figure of a black-and-orange Oriole in the center. Jim told me to pin it to the lapel because without it I wouldn't be allowed on the field, in the press box or in the locker rooms. I pinned it on my windbreaker, then mentioned I didn't have any warm clothes. Murray said he didn't either, so we asked the conceirge where the nearest department store was and he said there was a Gimbel's three blocks from the hotel. The snowfall had stopped but a steady, cold rain had replaced it. I grabbed Jim by the arm and guided him down the sidewalk, and past a construction site that was between the Hilton and the department store. A renovation of downtown Baltimore and its famous waterfront district was in progress and the streets in the neighborhood were torn up. I didn't want another rusty-sprinkler-pipe-at-Cal-State-Fullerton incident. We could have used a couple of hard hats in the heavy equipment zone, or at least an umbrella, but we made it to Gimbel's and bought two flannel pullover shirts.

When we got back to the hotel, officials announced that Game 1 had been postponed. Left and right fields in Memorial

Stadium were flooded and more snow was forecast by game time. This meant there would be no day off after Game 2.

We'd have to fly to Pittsburgh on Friday morning, the same day as Game 3 at Three Rivers Stadium. But the rainout gave Jim a chance to have some fun with the city of Baltimore. A quote in the *Baltimore Sun* read, "the planning for the invasion of Normandy pales in comparison to what major league teams do in advance of a World Series." Jim quipped, "German Field Marshal Von Rundstedt would be glad to hear that." Another line called the Series "a clash between cities where people work with their hands and get dirt under their fingernails" and it more than hinted that it was a refreshing change the hated Yankees, and also the Dodgers, Reds and Red Sox weren't involved.

Thomas Boswell of the *Washington Post* gushed, "The two best teams, the two hottest teams, and the two freshest and most interesting teams in baseball have made it to the World Series. That does not often happen."

Murray countered with, *"It's the hard hat World Series, two teams from the other side of the tracks. A truck driver's delight, a blue collar job.*

"This one's for the lunch pail crowd, for the guys who eat with their hats on and call the wife 'the old lady.' Baltimore and Pittsburgh (better known as "Bawlmer and Pittsbaarrrg"), two towns that talk out of the sides of their mouth, citadels of the working stiff. These aren't cities. They're just kind of complicated truck stops. Baltimore is like every town across the bay from a great city—like Oakland and Brooklyn, it suffers from a massive inferiority complex. The team is even owned by a lawyer from Washington. The State Department doesn't recognize the place. U.S. Senators pull the shades passing through. Cabinet officials won't go there even if they knew where it was."

Jim ended the column with a salute to Mark Belanger, the Orioles shortstop who was an excellent fielder but a poor hitter. Murray's angle was that you didn't have to be Babe Ruth or Mickey Mantle to make it to the World Series.

131

Belanger's batting average in 1979 was .167. He hit .206 in 1977 and went all the way up to .228 in 1978. The headline on the column read, *"The Shortstop Hits .200 and So Does the Town."*

October 10—The bus rolled through the wet streets of the suburbs as the sun tried to break through the hanging storm clouds. Its rays shone through the windows on the driver's side, sunning the flower of American sports journalism, then it disappeared into the gray. The bus passed blocks of row houses, all painted the same color, brown. Each house had the same front porch and children played on the steps or splashed in the puddles on the sidewalk.

I imagined that these houses might have been built early in the century, maybe at the same time Babe Ruth was growing up in Baltimore.

The bus smelled like a damp sweater or a wet dog. The seats were hard and the upholstery was frayed. On the front it said "CHARTER" and every seat was taken. Typewriters and briefcases were stuffed in the overhead compartments and under the seats. There was a lot of chatter and a genuine anticipation of getting the 1979 World Series started. The driver turned on the heater because it was cold, and it would get colder by the time Mike Flanagan threw the first pitch at 8:37 p.m.

The bus pulled into the parking lot of Memorial Stadium, the Grand Old Lady of 33rd Street, a park that had welcomed big league baseball in 1954 when the St. Louis Browns moved to Baltimore and changed their name to Orioles. It was also the home field for pro football's Baltimore Colts. Murray waited until all the passengers had filed out, then I helped him down the steps. Hubert Mizell of the *St. Petersburg Times*, Furman Bisher of the *Atlanta Journal*, Art Spander of the *San Francisco Examiner* and Edwin Pope of the *Miami Herald* stood by. "Everything OK, Jim?" Mizell asked. The columnists who had known Jim for years were concerned about their friend. Murray put both feet on the ground and said in a relieved voice, "Yes, thanks." We all walked to the press gate, which was also the players' entrance. I told Jim that it was Gate E2. Murray said, "Hey, Etchebarren, they named the gate after you." As we walked, Jim told the story about when catcher Andy Etchebarren became a full-time player for the Orioles in 1966, his teammates would kid him about Gate E2. When a catcher made an error, E2 was recorded in the official scorer's book.

The Pirates were in the middle of batting practice, so we followed a group of writers into the Pittsburgh dugout on the first base side of the field where Chuck Tanner and his coach, Bob Skinner, watched Willie Stargell, then Dave Parker, launch high fly balls over the right-field fence. Skinner chewed tobacco and he must have sat on the bench for some time because there was a large pool of tobacco spit on the floor. I tried to get close enough to Tanner to hear what he was saying but didn't realize until too late that I was standing in the brown juice. Dan Hafner once said that Herman Franks, who had managed the Giants and the Cubs, was the worst with tobacco. He chewed it while he talked and when he'd spit, the stains would get all over the front of his white uniform.

After the Pirates finished, we walked over to the third base dugout where Earl Weaver had made an appearance. The Orioles manager, known for his fiery disposition, which he displayed prominently in arguments with umpires and even his own players, was in a refreshingly pleasant mood. He was upbeat and smiling as he sat with one leg crossed over the other and his hat tilted back on his head.

Weaver confidently gave his assessment of the Series and what he expected from his team, which was a victory, although he wouldn't predict how many games it would take to win it. He said the Pirates were too good a team to be so bold. He confidently announced his pitching rotation. Flanagan would start the first game, followed by Palmer in Game 2 and McGregor in Game 3 at Pittsburgh.

The Orioles had several players from the Los Angeles area on their roster including infielder Rich Dauer, who played for Rod Dedeaux at USC; first baseman and designated hitter Eddie

Murray was from Locke High School; and catcher Rick Dempsey grew up in Woodland Hills and played ball for Crespi High in Encino. Tim Foli, who had come to the Pirates in a trade with the New York Mets in April, was also from the San Fernando Valley. The acquisitions of Foli, and then third baseman Bill Madlock from the Giants at midseason, had helped stabilize the Pittsburgh infield, and both players contributed with their bats, hitting .295 and .291, respectively.

As Weaver spoke, Howard Cosell entered the dugout with a camera crew and made himself at home on the bench, sitting next to the Orioles manager. Cosell, a commentator for ABC's *Monday Night Baseball* games with Bob Uecker, once said that he preferred football over baseball because he thought baseball was boring, but his opinion didn't stop him from being the center of attention in the dugout. Howard was on the scene, so now the Series could officially begin. He wore a brown trench coat, like the one Humphrey Bogart wore in *Casablanca*, and puffed on a big cigar as he talked to Weaver. Irv Brodsky, one of ABC's publicists, had arranged for Howard to have his own private box at the Series, in both cities. Murray once ran into Cosell in the press box at the Coliseum during halftime of a Raiders game. Howard complained to Jim about how he hated working for ABC and wanted to get out of his *Monday Night Football* obligation. After the game resumed, I said to Jim that Cosell sounded genuinely unhappy. But Murray said, "Don't believe a word of it. He loves it!"

A large buffet had been prepared for the media in the press room, which in Baltimore was called the Birdseed Room. It was nice to get in out of the frosty air and have dinner. It was the first time I ever had crabcakes and oysters, both delicacies in Baltimore. We stayed in the Birdseed Room until just before game time, then went out to our seats, which were in the field level stands behind home plate. The writers from National League cities had to sit there while those from American League towns got the warmer seats in the press box. Murray's Law of finding a seat and sitting in it until you're told to move would not work this time. But when the Series moved to Pittsburgh, the seating would be reversed and the National League writers would get the press box seats. It was 41 degrees when Mike Flanagan threw his first pitch for a strike.

The Orioles, aided by Doug DeCinces' two-run home run, scored five runs in the first inning off Pirates right-hander Bruce Kison, and the runs were enough for Flanagan, who pitched an undistinguished yet effective 11-hitter for a 5-4 win. In the fifth inning, Murray decided to go back into the Birdseed Room and write his column. It had become so cold that my feet started to hurt through my thin socks and loafers.

Jim wrote again in longhand and I retyped it, about three pages double spaced. A company called SportsCom, which had replaced Western Union typists in most big-league press boxes, sent the column via a Telecopier machine to the paper and it made deadline in plenty of time. I checked with the copy desk to make sure there were no questions and when I told Jim everything was all right, he said, "Well, we fooled them again."

October 11—Game 2 was delayed an hour by an icy rainfall. When it finally started, it was so cold that most of the writers who had seats outside stayed in the warm nest of the Birdseed Room and watched the game on television. Jim Palmer started for the O's and Eddie Murray homered, but in the ninth inning, with the game tied, 2-2, Weaver brought in his closer, Don Stanhouse. Stanhouse worked at a pace that had three speeds—slow, slower and crawl. Weaver called him "Fullpack" because Earl could smoke a pack of cigarettes in the time it took Stanhouse to complete his pitching assignment. Stanhouse, with his wild curly hair that stuck out from under his black cap, scraped the mound with his foot, stared in to get the sign from Rick Dempsey, then backed off the rubber, wiped his brow, and blew on his pitching hand. It seemed like he took a minute between pitches. Deadlines were in jeopardy all over America. "Throw the damn ball," someone in the room shouted. With Ed Ott on second base, pinch-hitter Manny

135

Sanguillen singled and Ott rounded third and scored to make it 3-2 Pirates. Kent Tekulve pitched a scoreless ninth to save the game for the winner, Don Robinson.

As the players quickly dressed to catch their planes to Pittsburgh, Chuck Tanner met with the media. "We're one and one here, and they only played .700 ball here," he said. "That's terrific." As he spoke, equipment managers and clubhouse attendants packed bats, gloves and uniforms into trunks. Some of the Orioles stood in line at a pizza stand to get a late-night snack, their suitcases stacked in rows outside the clubhouse. A few of the writers would fly to Pittsburgh that night but the majority, including Murray and myself, would make the 200-mile trip the next morning.

October 12—The Allegheny Airlines 727 lifted from the runway at 10 a.m. and headed northwest to the Steeltown. "Pittsbaarrrg," Murray said as our cab headed to the airport. "I'm in Pittsbaarrrg, Ma, and it's rainin'." Jim said that was the answer a foggy Ernie "The Rock" Durando gave to his cornermen when, after being floored by a straight right, his trainer asked, "Hey Rock, do you know where you are?"

The plane was filled to capacity and after the pilot turned off the FASTEN SEAT BELT sign, Stan Musial, the great St. Louis Cardinal first baseman and a boyhood hero of mine, got out of his seat and walked up the aisle. "Whatya say, whatya say, whatya say," Musial said as he greeted Rick Talley, who had been a columnist in Chicago and now was writing for the *L.A. Daily News*. Musial saw Jim and Murray stood up. He introduced me to Musial and it was a thrilling moment, one that I never expected, or will ever forget.

We landed at Pittsburgh International Airport, a few miles outside the city in the countryside. We stepped out of the terminal and, just as Jim had said, it was raining. The soggy, cold weather had followed us to western Pennsylvania and would have an effect on that night's game.

As we rode in a cab through a forest, I saw something that I

had seen on the outskirts of Baltimore. There was a small ceme-
tery alone on the roadside with old grave markers and headstones.
There wasn't a church or other buildings nearby, so I guessed that
the plots had been there a long time, even since the Civil War.

The cab dropped us at our hotel, the Point Park Hilton, which
overlooked the spot where the Allegheny and the Monongahela
rivers meet to form the Ohio River. Barges and boats sailed on the
Ohio and I could see Three Rivers Stadium across a bridge in the
foggy distance. On one of the downtown skyscrapers, a large
black-and-gold sign hung from a bank of windows that said, "Beat
'Em Bucs."

The bus to the ballpark was scheduled to leave at 6 p.m., and
when I went to collect Murray, he was on the phone with Gerry.
There was sad news from L.A. Rodney Brown had died in
Michigan and Gerry would leave that night for her brother's
funeral. Jim hung up the phone and gathered his jacket and briefcase. He fought back tears, saying to himself, "Poor Rodney."

On the field at Three Rivers, Jim attempted to interview
Eddie Murray but he couldn't get much out of the reluctant-to-talk
Orioles first baseman. Most of his answers came in one word or
silence. Eddie was only 23 years old and it was unusual for a
player that young to have such a sour attitude and estranged relationship with the press. Jim said you had to think it was something
else, maybe shyness or a family problem, that kept Eddie from
talking.

The Murray on Murray column didn't work, so Jim said,
"Let's go to Plan B." And that night, Plan B was to see what would
happen in the game.

Three Rivers Stadium was a circular park with a synthetic tar-
tan surface, as thin as outdoor carpeting. You could bounce a
baseball on it as high as your head. It was similar to Riverfront
Stadium in Cincinnati, a multipurpose facility with cement
facades that could accommodate both baseball and football.

Three Rivers was also the home park of the Pittsburgh
Steelers.

As we walked off the field, it started to rain lightly, and after 2½ innings the game was stopped for 67 minutes. It gave me a chance to see the Pirates' stadium club, a fabulous room called the Allegheny Club that was dedicated to the team's proud baseball history. It was a luxurious place, with views of the city that included our hotel at Point Park. Inside was a large piece of the left-center field wall from old Forbes Field, where the Pirates played until 1970. There was a memorial to Babe Ruth's 714th home run, which he hit at Forbes in his last big-league at-bat. And pictures of Big Poison and Little Poison—the Waner brothers Lloyd and Paul—and Ralph Kiner and Pie Traynor. Outside were statues of Honus Wagner, Roberto Clemente and Wilver Stargell.

The rain stopped and the groundskeepers brushed the water off the green carpet. Sister Sledge's "We Are Family," the Pirates' theme song, echoed from the right-field foul pole to the upper deck in left.

"We are family, I've got all my sisters with me" drove the fans to their feet as John Candelaria took the mound to resume Game 3. He would face Scott McGregor, the only left-handed player for the Orioles that night. Earl Weaver would send an all-right-handed attack against Candelaria, the Candy Man.

Backup shortstop Kiko Garcia had replaced Belanger and he delivered a four-hit performance that included a bases-loaded triple, while Benny Ayala, who had played in just 34 games in 1979, slugged a two-run home run. McGregor pitched 9 innings and gave up 9 hits, and the Orioles coasted to an 8-4 win, taking a 2-1 lead in the Series. After the game, the writers compared Garcia to Bucky Dent and Brian Doyle, the little-known New York Yankees who rose from anonymity to lead the Bronx Bombers to the 1978 American League pennant and a World Series win over the Dodgers.

Murray wrote, *"The Pittsburgh manager tries to win games the way Hitler tried to win wars, the way Grant took Richmond and the Indians took Custer. He just keeps throwing fresh troops into the breach, hang the attrition. Unlike Field Marshal Von*

Tanner, Earl Weaver appears to be an old softy who plays his pets. You'd think a lifetime .238 hitter would have to be related to the manager to get a start in a World Series game. But Weaver puts John Lowenstein in left field every chance he gets, leaving such a proven big league and Series performer as Lee May languishing on the bench. Weaver has a relief pitcher named Don Stanhouse, whose lifetime major league record is—get this—29-48. But Earl can't wait to get him in the game, possibly to make that record worse.

Meteorologically and artistically (11 errors so far), this World Series is a disaster. They try to play it in weather that would ground the Luftwaffe. But it's been a second-guessers' paradise."

October 13—When we arrived in the press box for Game 3, Jim had a seat but there wasn't one for me. Mel Durslag, the popular columnist for the *L.A. Herald-Examiner*, was nice enough to give me his so that I could sit next to Murray. I asked, "Where's Durslag going to sit?" Jim said, "Don't worry about Melvin, he'll be taken care of."

For Game 4, Durslag was not in sight, so we sat in the same seats, next to Jim's good friend, Blackie Sherrod, a columnist for the *Dallas Times Herald*, and Dave Anderson and Joe Durso of the *New York Times*. In the 1970s, Pittsburgh underwent a transformation from an industrial rivertown (steel and coal) to a more modern city that offered new business and cultural opportunities. It had avoided becoming part of the depressed and jobless Rust Belt of the industrial northeast. The old staples of steel mills, mines and the railroad had been replaced by a renaissance of high technology, biomedics, banking and services. Many of the downtown buildings that had been blackened with soot and grime from decades of polluted air were being sandblasted and painted. An old church that was under renovation near the stadium was half black and half white. The Pittsburgh Symphony would play sold-out performances and had gained a reputation as one of the better orchestras in the world.

The national anthem for Game 4 was to be sung by an opera singer. Even though it was a Saturday day game, the windows of the press box were closed because of the cold air. As the woman began, "O say, can you see," Blackie inched away from the glass. "We better stand back when she hits the high note," he said.

The Pirates quickly got out to a 4-0 lead and were ahead 6-3 in the eighth inning when Tanner summoned Tekulve from the bullpen. Weaver had anticipated this move and a slight smile came across his face when he saw the submarine-style pitcher take the mound. The bases were loaded and Weaver had a trap set for Tekulve. He had saved his left-handed pinch-hitters for precisely this moment. Up to bat came Lowenstein, who doubled. Next was Billy Ed Smith. He walked. Terry Crowley ripped a double and the Orioles had the lead, 7-6.

Baltimore added insult to injury when Weaver had pitcher Tim Stoddard bat, the same player whose loud radio interfered with Murray's attempt to send his column at Anaheim Stadium. Stoddard didn't have a hit in the big leagues and Weaver instructed him to take the first two strikes. But the ex-basketball player from North Carolina State swung at the first pitch and singled over third base to drive in a run. The Orioles won 9-6 and now led 3-1, with Flanagan, Palmer and McGregor set to start the final three games.

Afterward, Weaver talked about his left-handed batters, saying he noticed something about Tekulve in Game 2. "He was eating our right-handers alive. That's why I didn't pinch-hit for them early on."

In the Pirates clubhouse, Tekulve was stretched out on a trunk, politely answering questions. He said he didn't think Weaver had saved his left-handers just for him. But when told what Weaver said, Tekulve bristled, "He's going to get blown out of a couple games waiting for me and I'm never going to get there."

The Pirates got 17 hits, a World Series record, but it was little consolation, and when Dave Parker was asked about his team's precarious position, he snapped, "Ain't too good, is it?"

Tanner tried to sound positive, saying, "We've had three-game winning streaks before." I walked Murray from the Pirates' clubhouse to the elevator and back to the press box. For the first time on the trip, the words didn't immediately come to him. He sat at a table and stared at a blank piece of drawing paper. He wrote a sentence in longhand, then stopped and crumpled the paper into a ball and started again. The angle for the column finally came and he wrote:

"Earl Weaver, a master of winning pots with short money by pasting together teams out of the want ads and the Yellow Pages, shrewdly hoarded his left-handed pinch-hitters. He was like a jockey who knows he has a lot of horse left under him. He let the Pirates open up a wide lead. In the eighth, he called the dealer, he faded the shooter. The Pirates had taken the field dressed, fittingly, in gold uniforms. The Orioles had drab gray. They wisely had their names on the back of their uniforms. They should have had their ranks and serial numbers, too.

"Well, the smart money is down to their last white chip. The Orioles are sitting there with stacks of blues and reds spilling all over the table, and grinning wickedly. They are like guys who came into town on a bus and broke the bank. They are like the janitor who won the lottery.

"The team that nobody wanted, nobody believed in, nobody bet on, won more games than any team in baseball and appears about to show the guys in the gold suits, as they have shown all of Baseball, that all that is gold does not glitter."

I typed Murray's handwritten work and gave it to the fellow from SportsCom, who waited patiently nearby. After he sent it to the sports department and had given it back to me, I asked Jim if he wanted to keep it, but, in a rare display of disgust, Murray said, "No, I never want to see it again."

The Pirates had provided a boxed lunch that consisted of two greasy pieces of cold chicken, an apple, a cookie and a soft drink, but Jim didn't eat it. I thought his anger came from being tired and upset over his brother-in-law's death. I said I was hungry so we ate dinner at the hotel with John Strege and Lyle Spencer of the *Herald-Examiner*. They had made plans to go to a nightclub called the 6:30 Club, and they invited me to join them. I asked Jim if he wanted to go, but he said, "No, you go with your friends." He was in a low mood from the long day, and although he would never say it, I had the feeling he hoped the Orioles would end the Series the next day and he could go home.

****

The 6:30 Club was a short walk from our hotel. On the way, we ran into Tom Lasorda and Steve Brener, the Dodgers' public relations director. The two men had been at the club and were walking back to the Hilton. The 6:30 Club was Pittsburgh's equivalent of P.J. Clarke's in New York City, a popular bar with the media and sports fans. But it was also a neighborhood watering hole, patronized by the city's working sector. The club's unique feature was that it stayed open until 6:30 in the morning. The entry way was actually a side door that seemed to be part of the masonry of the building, like a speakeasy's entrance during 1930s Prohibition. A small sign above the door in black letters read "6:30."

The bar area was full as were two other rooms, and it took a few minutes to order a beer. I recognized many faces from the game that day and even though we had to stand, it was a fun and relaxed atmosphere. Some people eventually sat down on the floor. I had a Iron City beer with John and Lyle and later asked one of the bartenders if I could buy a can to go, to take back to L.A. for Marilyn White. He was reluctant at first but I told him who I was and what it was for, and he gave me a can. It had a team picture of the Pittsburgh Steelers on the front. I knew some of the writers would try to stay until morning, to boast that they closed the 6:30 Club, a tradition if you come to Pittsburgh to cover a sports event, but after another beer I headed back to the Hilton. It was a nice walk in the cool early-morning air.

October 14—For the first time in a week, the sun shone on

Sunday, but more sadness would darken the Series. Chuck Tanner's mother, Anne, had died suddenly early that morning. She was 70 and had been under care for a stroke that she had suffered a week earlier, and when Chuck called before the game to see how she was, he was given the news of her death.

He faced a packed press conference and said, "I knew I was doing something [staying with the team] she'd want me to do. She knew this was my life. I know she's in Heaven. I know she's happy. It's going to happen to all of us some day so let's enjoy ourselves and give it our best and be strong. I can be strong."

Tanner's inspiration lifted his team, and behind Jim Rooker whom Tanner had named at the last minute to replace an ailing Bruce Kison, the Pirates scored four runs off Mike Flanagan and three more off Don Stanhouse to win, 7-1.

Rooker pitched five strong innings and Stargell, Parker and Madlock, who had four hits, led the Pittsburgh offense.

A floral arrangement of yellow carnations and black ribbons was sent to Tanner and the team by Sister Sledge. But the atmosphere in the clubhouse was anything but funereal. The Pirates had pulled together around Tanner and Stargell, the way a family would embrace a patriarch in a time of trouble. The Pirates were touched by the way their manager had put aside his grief to lead them. "He walked very tall today," Stargell said. "I really saw something in that man. I could tell he was hurting but he wouldn't let it show because he didn't want it to reflect on the team."

The Pirates lovingly called Stargell "Pops" and Murray wrote, *"He looks like what you'd imagine Uncle Remus looked like, a great kindly giant of a man with sad eyes. When he talks in that deep bass voice, you'd imagine that's how God sounded like talking to Moses. He may be the most popular man to play baseball since Babe Ruth. Booing him would be like booing Bambi, a Red Cross truck at a flood. He could crush a Volkswagen, lift a freight car or swing a railroad tie with one hand. In another time, you would imagine him driving steel—more steel than anyone in the rail gang."*

143

Jim was in a better mood after the game. The Series had tightened up, the Pirates had renewed vigor and there was a lot to write about. We were headed back to Baltimore in the morning with the Orioles clinging to a 3-2 lead. I packed my suitcase, carefully placing in it souvenirs that included a Pirates pennant, the can of beer and my Series pin. I looked out the picture window of my room to the view of the city's brightly lit skyline. The boats and the barges, with their running lights blinking in the dark, sailed down the Ohio River under bridges and overpasses, and it was a pretty sight. I liked Pittsburgh, and for a moment, I was sorry that we had to leave.

Chapter Nine

The Family s Hour

"You've got to be careful if you don't know where you're going 'cause you might not get there."

—Yogi Berra

The good news was that Indian Summer had finally arrived in Maryland and we didn't have to wear our funky flannel shirts anymore. The bad news, though, was we had lost our rooms at the Hilton in Baltimore because a convention had come into town while the Series was in Pittsburgh. The National League writers had been relocated to the Cross Keys Inn in Columbia, Maryland, an industrial park town between Baltimore and Washington, D.C., and about 20 miles from Memorial Stadium.

I rented a car and drove to Columbia. Jim couldn't read the map so I held it in one hand and steered with the other. I thought, foolishly as it turned out, *I can find this place. I'm from L.A. and had driven its freeways since I was sixteen. What can be so hard about maneuvering the Beltways of Baltimore?* Well, plenty as I found out. The exit signs weren't street names like Ventura Boulevard or Vermont Avenue or Moraga Drive. Most of the

145

streets were one-way avenues, and the exits were designated by either numbers or letters.

After driving once around the Belt, I found the right exit and we arrived at the hotel while it was still daylight. The main building was two stories tall and we had to use the stairs to get to our rooms. The light in the stairwell was dim and it wasn't much better in the hallway. Murray was unsure of his footing on the stairs, especially when he went down, so I took him by arm each time. I saw John Strege, Lyle Spencer and Gordon Verrell of the *Long Beach Press-Telegram* arrive, then Rick Talley. Although we accepted our lodging situation, we were dismayed about being that far from town. I told Jim that I didn't see Mel Durslag, and Murray said, "I'm sure Melvin has made a call to Barron Hilton."

That night, the L.A. contingent ate dinner in the hotel's restaurant and capped it off with a drink in the bar. Murray enjoyed the company of beat writers as much as he did that of columnists, owners and general managers. In fact, he admired the younger reporters because of their enthusiasm and energy.

He always had time to talk to them and would go out of his way if one needed a favor or advice. The happiest I ever saw Murray was on a street corner in Las Vegas. He was there for the Muhammad Ali-Larry Holmes fight and had joined up with a group of writers outside Caesar's Palace. As he crossed the street with Budd Schulberg, author of *On the Waterfront* and *The Harder They Fall*, Eddie Pope, Tom Callahan of *Time* magazine, and other friends, a look that said "life can't get better than this" was on his face. I noticed it in a glance but it's a mental snapshot I'll always remember.

October 16—We entered Memorial Stadium through the Etchebarren Gate and as we walked into the Birdseed Room, Irv Brodsky stopped Jim and asked if he wanted to watch the game from the private box that was reserved for Howard Cosell. The suite was on the press box level down the left field line and would be empty because Cosell would be in the ABC broadcast booth. Jim took Brodsky up on the offer and we had a suite to ourselves.

Jim Palmer faced John Candelaria and both pitchers got their teams through six innings without giving up a run. But Pittsburgh broke through with two in the top of the seventh, then scored two more in the eighth inning. Kent Tekulve picked up for Candelaria in the seventh and pitched three scoreless innings to secure a 4-0 win, and the Pirates thus dramatically tied the Series, 3-3, forcing a Game 7. It was later revealed that Candelaria had pulled a muscle in his side while he warmed up before the game.

Murray wrote his column in the ABC suite and afterward we walked back to the press room to send it to the sports department.

"BALTIMORE—You've got to like a fighter who gets up. You've got to like a horse who comes from behind. You've got to like a guy who raises with his last buck. You've got to like the unsinkable Molly Brown. And you've got to like the Pittsburgh Pirates. You've got to throw in with a guy who's sitting there with both legs broken and says, 'Never mind me, look after those other guys.' Two days ago the Pittsburgh Pirates were out of this tournament. They had just lost two games in the most humiliating way possible. They piled up 3-0 and 4-0 leads and got tackled from behind. The Orioles appeared to be dancing on their graves. The autopsy would show they died of shock. The Pirates were like the fighter sitting on the stool battered and floored, the ref looking at them quizzically and asking them where, or even who, they were, and they said, 'Just point me at 'em. I'll moida the bum!' The Pirates came out throwing punches. As long as they could hear the other guy breathing, they would aim at the sound."

The Pittsburgh clubhouse was jubilant. Dave Parker bellowed, "Man, it's five-card stud showdown now."

"Keep doing it Bucs—gotta keep doing it—gotta do it one more time," cheered second baseman Phil Garner, who went 2 for 3 to improve his Series average to .524. He also helped execute the Pirates infield's ninth double play and robbed Benny Ayala of a hit late in the game. The Pirates had beaten Flanagan and Palmer. But could they draw Trip Aces and beat Scott McGregor? As Murray and I walked out of the ballpark to the car, the air was quiet and cool. The Baltimore faithful had slipped into the night to wait and see how their beloved Birds would play their hand in Game 7.

On the way back to the Cross Keys Inn, I made a turn off the Beltway to Interstate 95 and thought I was headed south but was actually driving north. The highway is a major artery into and out of Washington from the northeast.

After about an hour, I started to see little waves on a large body of water on the right side of the car. I mentioned this to Jim, and Murray said, "I don't think we're going the right way, John."

The water was the shoreline of Chesapeake Bay, but I wasn't convinced we were lost. I stubbornly drove on until we passed a road sign that said "Philadelphia 60 Miles." I had almost driven to Delaware and Murray started to chuckle as I turned the car around. We stopped at a liquor store and I got directions back to Columbia. Like the rusty-pipe leg injury, the statute of limitations didn't run out on our side trip to Philadelphia, as Jim teasingly liked to call it.

October 17—I awoke the next morning with a painful sore throat and a fever. Too many cold, wet nights at the ballpark, not enough sleep, too much hotel room service food, too much 6:30 Club, too many rich oysters and crabcakes in the Birdseed Room. I felt lousy but I pulled myself together and got Murray to the game.

There's nothing like Game 7 of the World Series. Billy Martin once said that winning it was not only the ultimate victory for a baseball team, but it was a barometer that showed which league was the better. Earl Weaver would put the Series in the hands of his last ace, Scott McGregor. The Pirates' hopes would ride with Jim Bibby, the third pitcher in Chuck Tanner's rotation, and then the manager would use whoever was left on the depleted staff, probably Bert Blyleven, and then prayed a worn-out Kent Tekulve would be there for him in the late innings. We got a ride to the ballpark with Rick Talley, for which I was grateful, and Jim wanted to sit in the ABC box again, but when we got to the suite, Irv Brodsky met us and said that because President Jimmy Carter would attend the game, the Secret Service would use the box as a command post for its agents. This meant we had to make the long walk back to the Birdseed Room. My throat was raw and I had run out of energy. I wanted to say, "Find me a place to lie down," but Brodsky and I escorted Murray to a seat in the press section in the stands. I probably should have told Jim I wasn't feeling well because he sensed something was wrong, but I kept it to myself. I bought a hot cup of coffee and I started feeling better after the game started.

The Orioles' fans, over 50,000 of them, got into the game on McGregor's first pitch. Their O-R-I-O-L-E-S spell-out reverberated around the field, and a wave circled the ballpark—right in the first inning. In the third, Baltimore took a 1-0 lead on a surprise home run by the light-hitting Rich Dauer. McGregor pitched stronger as the game progressed and he looked unhittable when he set the Pirates down in the fifth inning on a variety of off-speed pitches and curve balls. Tanner squeezed four innings out of Bibby and replaced him with Don Robinson in the fifth. With two out, Doug DeCinces singled and McGregor walked.

Tanner called time and brought in Grant Jackson, who got Al Bumbry to foul out.

In the sixth, Tanner got the break he needed when, with one out, Bill Robinson singled off Kiko Garcia's glove at short. Willie Stargell slowly walked to the plate and stepped into the batter's box with a man on base.

Earlier, Stargell had doubled and singled, but the bases were empty both times, and then the Pirates stranded him. Willie was hitting .400 for the Series and Tanner saw this at-bat as his best chance to score against McGregor.

Chuck cupped his hands to his mouth and yelled, "Come on, Pops." Every player in the Pirates dugout and bullpen was on his feet, clapping hands and pleading for their captain to hit the ball. The Orioles' players and fans cheered just as hard for McGregor. Weaver knew that Stargell liked the ball low and he yelled from the dugout to Dempsey to give McGregor a high target. Either Rick couldn't hear Weaver's instructions or McGregor missed the sign, because the pitch was down. Stargell swung and hit a deep fly into the brisk Baltimore night that carried into the Pirates bullpen, for a 2-1 lead. That, effectively, was the Series. Pittsburgh scored 2 more runs in the ninth and Tekulve shut down the Orioles to save the win for Jackson.

The Pirates had become only the fourth team in baseball history to win a World Series after trailing 3 games to 1. "With Flanagan, Palmer and McGregor coming right in line, you had to like the chances," a disappointed Weaver said afterward. But in reality, the Pirates outpitched the Orioles in the last three games. They gave the Most Valuable Player award to Stargell, who graciously accepted it. "There are no words to say what this team means to me," he said. "I started this family thing because it was something we felt typified our club. It wasn't meant to be fancy or sassy. I know they have to give the MVP award to one person but I wish I could give it to everybody on the team."

"Who's the MVP?" asked Bill Robinson. "Stargell? Oh, good. He's something. He deserves it."

Willie had 12 hits, 7 RBIs, 3 home runs and became the first player to have 7 extra-base hits in a Series. "What can I say about a man who's going to the Hall of Fame," replied Tanner afterward. "He's one of the greatest ever."

President Carter entered the euphoric Pirates clubhouse. He congratulated Tanner and posed for photos as he and the manager held the World Series trophy above their heads.

I got as many quotes as I could for Murray, who wrote as fast as he could in longhand. I typed it on the drawing paper and it was one of the best columns on deadline that he had ever composed, as good as those he'd written when he could see.

"BALTIMORE—All his life, Scott McGregor dreamed of pitching the seventh game of the World Series. OK, I can relate to that. But I wonder if he ever dreamed of serving up a low breaking ball to Willie Stargell and dreamed of watching it—and the World Series—sail over the right-center field fence. I'm a big expert on dreams—and in every dream I ever had no one ever hit

off me with the Series on the line. I never missed a putt on the 18th hole of the Open. Dempsey missed me with all those left hooks and no one touched me as I went 80 yards into the end zone against Notre Dame. The Pittsburgh Pirates are champions of the whole world because dreams don't come true. Memorial Stadium was the boulevard of broken dreams for Scotty McGregor and the Baltimore Orioles. You don't dream of Grant Jackson, of all people, being the winning pitcher against you. In a proper dream, you beat Koufax.

"The drama of the 38-year-old slugger driving the 5-year-old kid's dream over the right-center field fence highlights a very good seventh game and made an incident to rank with legends of Ruth and Dean and Stengel and Gehrig in Series lore. The World Series came to a merciful end at 11:28 Wednesday night. It dies of exposure. It was as much fun most of the time as being torpedoed in the Murmansk Run. It was Stargell's World Series and will doubtless remain so in baseball history. If Willie had a dream of hitting the home run that won a World Series as a kid, it's so long ago he can't remember it.

"The Orioles said the old man hit a good pitch. They lost the Series in the most shocking way possible. Sitting on a 3-1 lead in games, they had the aces of their staff, three stars to get one win— Mike Flanagan, Jim Palmer and Scott McGregor. Their batters managed two runs in their last three games. It's doubtful if that occurred in Scott McGregor's dream at age five.

"In a world that increasingly belongs to the young, it's nice there is a man they call 'Pops' in the clubhouse, the wise old vet who had popped up, struck out or bounced weakly when it didn't matter, who finally could call on eyes that need glasses to read and recognize a home-run ball one more time.

"It's too bad he had to poke a hole in the kid's dream. But us old folks can dream too."

We had to wait in the pressroom for about 40 minutes after Jim's column had been sent to the paper because the Baltimore police had to clear about 1,000 fans out of the ballpark. They had

151

run onto the field to rip up the bases and sections of the outfield grass. As they did this, they jubilantly shouted out the O-R-I-O-L-E-S cheer. It was almost as if Baltimore had won. We arrived back at the Cross Keys Inn about 2 a.m. and it would be only a few hours before we would have to leave for Dulles International airport. The good news was we were going home.

In the morning, my sore throat was better and the fever was gone. Rick Talley, who was on our flight to Los Angeles, volunteered to drive to Reston, Virginia. Jim talked him into a quick sightseeing trip through Washington. "Scheib wants to the see the Capitol Building."

I had to sit in the back seat on top of one of the suitcases, but the hard ride was worth it. We passed the Capitol, the White House, and other historic buildings and monuments. As we drove across Potomac River, I looked back and saw the red brick buildings of Georgetown. At Dulles, the Concorde had landed from Paris and it taxied past our shuttle as we headed out to our plane, a United Airlines DC-10.

As we waited to board, everyone in the shuttle watched a ground crew work on the left wing of the plane. Earlier that year, a DC-10 had crashed after it had taken off from Chicago's O'Hare Airport. The DC-10 fleet was grounded until an investigation found that a pylon on one of the engines had broken loose and caused the engine to fall off. Some people in the back of the shuttle called out, "Tighten up that pylon."

We flew home in first class again, with glasses of champagne and carnations in our lapels. I saw the Mississippi River out the window as we flew over the Illinois-Missouri border.

Ted Murray picked us up at the airport and he dropped me off at my apartment. I was exhausted and for the first time in 11 days, I slept all night.

The next morning I weighed myself and I'd lost 11 pounds. But it was a diet I would gladly go on again because, for a young journalist and baseball fan, traveling to the World Series with Jim Murray was a joy of a lifetime.

I was scheduled to work in the office that night. I gave Marilyn White her can of Iron City beer. Bob Lochner, a senior editor in sports, stopped me in the hallway and complimented Murray on the "terrific job" he'd done at the Series. "He was right on it," Lochner said about Jim's column after the Pirates had tied the Series, 3-3. His comment made me feel proud.

Murray's Series postscript read, *"It was a better World Series than it had a right to be. On paper it looked like an agony fight. Strictly an undercard match in baseball history, a plating race. But a World Series that stars Willie Stargell, like any movie which stars Redford, moves up in class, and is a main-event. The Baltimore Orioles, such a collection of mystery guests they should have played in masks, almost stole it. But the majestic figure of Wilver Dornel Stargell, the nearest thing to Babe Ruth this generation has seen, wouldn't let them. He elevated himself and the Series in the process."*

Bill Shirley called me into his office. "Scheibe, I'm anxious to see your expense report." I told him I'd have it for him as soon as possible, but I called Jim first to see if he was going to include in his expenses the flannel shirts we had bought during the snowstorm. He said he wasn't sure, and the sound in his voice indicated he probably wouldn't, so I decided not to include it in mine. I hung it in a closet and hardly wore it afterward, a gaudy souvenir from a baseball game.

"But now the old red light is slanting swiftly, the crowd is waiting tense and silent, already with a touch of sorrow, resignation, and the winter in their hearts, for summer's over, the game is ending, and October has come again, has come again."

—Thomas Wolfe

Chapter Ten

Out of the Darkness

*"A life is not important except in the impact
it has on other lives."*
—Jackie Robinson

"Pick up the pace, pick it up!" Avrum Dansky shouted. It was a college football Saturday, the busiest day, and night, of the week for the sports department. Dansky would yell at himself when he thought he had fallen behind in his work. He retyped each summary for every game played that day, from the contests in the Big Ten and Pac-10 to the Ivy League and Southeastern Conference, a monumental task that took him from about noon until the last game ended, which on most football Saturdays was 11 p.m.

Avrum could have taken the easy route and sent the summaries, which came from the wire services, straight to the linotypists, but he insisted that each one be written in *Times* style, which in this case was Dansky's own style.

Avrum liked to put in little nuggets of information for the reader that the wire services didn't provide.

It also gave him the opportunity to make sure the yardage

155

totals were correct. It would irritate the writers at a Rams or UCLA game when Dansky would call the press box to tell them their stats were wrong. "On your 'How They Scored,' you can't have a ten-yard field goal," or "Harmon's passing yardage on UCLA's first touchdown drive doesn't add up."

With the baseball season over, Murray's attention turned to football, although he mixed in two baseball columns with others on the Rams and the USC and UCLA football squads. The first was on pitcher Rick Sutcliffe. The Dodgers had called a press conference at Little Joe's, an Italian restaurant in the Chinatown district downtown, to announce that Sutcliffe had been named the National League's Rookie of the Year. Peter O'Malley, who had taken over the leadership of the team following his father's death, attended, as did Tom Lasorda and several players including Don Sutton. Sutcliffe, a tall, rangy right-hander, had won 17 games in 1979 and was the first of three consecutive Dodger pitchers to win the Rookie of the Year award. Reliever Steve Howe was named in 1980 and Fernando Valenzuela would win it in 1981.

The second baseball column was on Howard Cosell, who was in Los Angeles for a *Monday Night Football* game at the Coliseum. Murray asked him about his reported dislike of baseball and of broadcasting its games. Cosell said he was resentful of the rap. "I object to its being an anomaly of law, because of its unique exception from the Constitution or the Bill of Rights, and I resent carpetbagger ownerships," he told Jim in a telephone interview. "But after the World Series, NBC sent word to its baseball crew that it wanted baseball presented to the public 'just the way Howard Cosell presented it in the World Series.'

"There were seventy different times during the World Series that the public met the players and the managers personally on camera and what came out of that was human identification. Everyone said it was going to be a dud, a so-what World Series, but what came out of it was eighty-six million viewers, more than had ever watched before. Dave Parker got a movie role as a result of those interviews.

"Willie Stargell became an institution. If that's disliking baseball, it's a peculiar form of it."

Murray wrote, *"[Cosell] is generous with his time. He logs more hours flying to charity luncheons, roasts, or hokey award banquets than any celebrity this side of Bob Hope. He is convivial. He likes a good cigar, a good vodka, and, above all, a good audience. He can read off from memory the numbers of the entire 1925 Notre Dame varsity—or recite Milton from memory. He likes his life."*

****

"What's happening in the real world, Scheib?" Murray asked when I picked him up to drive to an interview with USC quarterback Paul McDonald at the campus' Howard Jones Field. Jim liked to compare a newspaper to a three-course dinner. The news section with its national and foreign stories was the meat and potatoes, the local news was the vegetables, and the sports section was the dessert.

On the national music chart, "Do Ya Think I'm Sexy?" by Rod Stewart, "Bad Girls" by Donna Summer and "My Sharona" by the Knack are in the Top Ten; thirteen of the sixty-two American hostages being held at the U.S. Embassy in Tehran, Iran, are released for medical and other humanitarian reasons; Afghanistan resistance fighters are supported by the United States with medical supplies, Stinger missiles and other small arms. Among these mujahideen or "holy warriors" is Osama bin Laden; the price of gasoline in California has dramatically jumped from $0.50 to nearly $1 a gallon; and the price of gold spikes at $500 an ounce. Major League Baseball tells Willie Mays that he must sever all ties with the game after he accepts a job with an Atlantic City hotel and casino. And Nancy Lopez is the leading money winner on the LPGA tour, earning over $187,000.

We arrived at USC and entered the campus from Jefferson Boulevard just as the Trojans were about to end their afternoon practice. It had been a nearly perfect autumn day in Los Angeles, the air was dry, the Santa Monica Mountains were visible from the ocean to Hollywood, and long shadows extended on the leaf-scattered walkways from the sycamores which had turned brown in the fall sun.

Murray walked down to Howard Jones Field, a new facility that had replaced Bovard Field as the football team's practice field, and watched from the sidelines as the first-string offense practiced in full pads against the starting defense. The ball was handed off to the fullback who hit the line off tackle and was thrown back for a loss. The offensive line coach stopped the play and addressed the left guard and tackle in a voice that sounded like a Marine drill sergeant's. "Listen, damn it, if you can't block, we'll get someone out here who can," he barked. His ire was directed at players on a team that was undefeated, had soundly beaten Notre Dame, 42-23, a week earlier in South Bend, Indiana, and was ranked in the top five in the polls. Nine USC players, including Anthony Muñoz and Brad Budde, would be drafted by NFL teams in 1980. Tailback Charles White would outpoint Billy Sims of Oklahoma in ballot votes to win the Heisman Trophy.

The coach called the same play and this time the fullback ran through a large hole on the left side for a sizable gain. "That's more like it," he muttered as another coach blew his whistle that signaled the end of practice.

The players gathered their gear and trotted off the field, and Coach John Robinson walked over to welcome Murray. Jim told Robinson that he was there to talk to McDonald and Robinson was pleased to hear it. "It doesn't matter if [Paul] goes on to play pro football or not, he's going to make a contribution to the community after he leaves here," Robinson said.

Tim Tessalone, the school's sports information director, escorted McDonald over to Jim and we all sat down on a bench outside Heritage Hall.

Although he was dressed in his practice uniform—white pants and yellow jersey—the senior looked more like a distance runner or a high jumper than a quarterback. He was tall and slender, with wavy brown hair, and left-handed—physical features that played into the angle Murray had in mind for his column.

Jim wondered why a gifted passer like Paul, who had been recruited by California and New Mexico, would choose a football program whose emphasis was on run, run and run again. Hadn't he heard of Mike Garrett, Anthony Davis, O.J. Simpson, Ricky Bell and Clarence Davis, Student Body Right and the Heisman Trophies?

"First of all," McDonald explained, "SC goes to the Rose Bowl a lot. Next, they told me they were going to change the whole emphasis here."

Murray wrote, *"They were going to let the quarterback out of the closet, is what they were going to do. They were going to let him come to the dance with the others. Coach John Robinson assured McDonald the position was no longer going to be just the office boy's. USC is not exactly an aerial circus now. But McDonald put the ball in the air 67 times in two games, USC-Notre Dame and USC-Cal.*

"And Paul McDonald, the thinking man's quarterback, came to the astonishing conclusion that the perfect spot for a quarterback to be was in the USC backfield."

"With all those Heismans running around," McDonald noted, "receivers tend to be wide open a lot. The other guys have to overplay the run, you see."

In a game against Arizona on November 3, McDonald improved his bid to become USC's first All-American at quarterback by passing for 380 yards and three touchdowns in the Trojans' 34-7 win at the Coliseum. He established a school record for passing yardage, breaking the single-game record set by Craig Fertig in 1964 of 371 yards, and set another school record of 25 completions in 35 attempts.

Murray continued, *"It's havoc for defenses that way. They not only have to watch for Student Body Right and Student Body Left, but now Student Body deep. At future alumni rallies, the colloquy may well turn out to be, 'Now let's see, who was the tailback the year Paul McDonald completed all those passes? Can't think of his name at the moment—but he won the Heisman Trophy.'"*

USC's offense was the envy of the college coaching world. It also had the Newport Beach alumni in a swoon, the Cardinal and Gold Club giddy with delight. The only blemish on the Trojans' 1979 record was a 21-21 tie with Stanford. "I'd like to have an offense like Southern Cal," said Earle Bruce at Ohio State. "They're the team of the century in mixing the run and the pass." Arkansas' Frank Broyles added, "The Trojans are awesome—with a most uncommon offense based on a combination of runs and passes. I don't know any coach who has done more than John Robinson with the combination."

Although the bread and butter of USC's offense was still the running game, Robinson had upgraded it to more of a pro-style attack. He was fortunate, though, to have the talent to execute his offensive strategy, and many of these players had been recruited by his predecessor, John McKay. When McKay left USC in 1976 for the NFL's Tampa Bay Buccaneers, he told his successor, "Robbie, the cupboard isn't bare." In addition to the nine players who would be drafted by NFL clubs, the team's underclassman included Ronnie Lott, Dennis Smith, Marcus Allen, Keith Van Horne, Jeff Fisher and Chip Banks.

It was mid-November and what little eyesight Murray had in his right eye was rapidly deteriorating away. At his home, he walked slowly through rooms and hung on to doorways. The cataract on his good eye had thickened considerably.

Our trips became short-range and to places that he was familiar with, such as the Coliseum. Still, his writing remained fresh and entertaining. He wrote superlative columns on UCLA's Freeman McNeil and the Rams' Fred Dryer and Larry Brooks.

We met McNeil in an office at UCLA's Pauley Pavilion, just down the hill and across Sunset Boulevard from Murray's house. As Jim sat down with McNeil, coach Terry Donahue stuck his head in the door. "Hey, that looks like a football player," he said, smiling at McNeil. Freeman was the other tailback in Los Angeles, a star on his team. but as a junior, he played in the shadow of USC's Charles White. Although they were nearly equals on the field, White and McNeil were opposites off the gridiron.

Freeman went to Banning High School in the harbor neighborhood of Wilmington near San Pedro. Charles grew up on the rough-and-tumble streets of San Fernando in the north San Fernando Valley. White was cocky and brash and boldly predicted when he enrolled at USC that he would win "a couple of Heismans." McNeil was reserved and soft-spoken. John Robinson said that Charles White was the toughest player he ever coached. McNeil was tough too, but in a less pretentious way. He rushed for 1,343 yards and 27 touchdowns and an L.A. City championship in his senior year at Banning High School. He was recruited by Notre Dame, Texas and USC, but he chose UCLA, which at the time ran the Veer offense, designed more for option-play quarterbacks than 30-carries-a-game tailbacks.

Murray asked McNeil if he ever thought he had made the wrong choice in schools. "At first, my first couple of games, I wished I had gone to the other place. I thought I had made a mistake. But as I grew with the team and into the program and we put in the I formation, I grew to like it here. Matter of fact, I always wanted to play on a team that would beat USC."

Jim wrote, *"The facts of the matter are Freeman McNeil would get a more rousing Heisman constituency if he played for Ohio State—or Penn State. Here he's Harry Steinfeldt or Earl Britton (who blocked for Red Grange). He's in the wrong place at the wrong time. His 1,276 yards for 10 games compares favorably to Charles White's 1,609 yards for 10 games. But, the regional bloc voting goes to one guy at a time. Charles White."*

McNeil would never win the Heisman but he would help the Bruins to a 20-17 victory over USC the next season. He was drafted in the first round by the New York Jets in 1981, No. 3 overall behind George Rogers and Lawrence Taylor, and would go on to have a solid 12-year career in the pros, a New York Jet all the way, rushing for over 1,000 yards in 1984 and 1985 and a Pro Bowl choice three times.

USC and UCLA had productive offenses, but their professional counterpart, the Rams, lacked one for most of 1979. With six games left in the regular season, Pat Haden went down in Seattle with a broken finger and his replacement, an inexperienced Vince Ferragamo, struggled to pick up the offense. Ray Malavasi brought in Bob Lee and Jeff Rutledge as stopgaps until Ferragamo became comfortable behind the center, but the team's running game was so inept it didn't matter who called the plays. Between them, Wendell Tyler and Cullen Bryant scored just 15 touchdowns, less than one a game, for the season.

In a game in late October against the mediocre New York Giants, the Rams scored just two touchdowns and lost 20-14. The custom at the Coliseum's press box was with 5 minutes left, the home team's publicist would lead the writers down the steps through the stands to the field where they would watch the game until it was over, then walk ahead of the players through the stadium's tunnel and to the dressing rooms. It was too risky to walk Jim down the seventy-five or so steps through a large crowd of fans, some of whom had been back and forth to the beer stands, so he went down the elevator and around the outside of the Coliseum to the locker rooms.

Murray described the Rams as *"a beautiful, finely tuned automobile—without wheels...a gorgeous bird that can't fly. It's not easy to lose to the New York Giants. Considering the disparity in personnel, the Rams had to plot their defeat carefully. One false move, one mistake, and they would have blown the Giants out of there, as they did a few years ago, 55-14. This is a team that needs a rearview mirror. Some of the Rams' best drives have been from their own 35 to their own 15. Billy Wilder would love the Rams. Like one of his dotty characters plying the waters of the bay stern-first, they blithely pretend to ignore that they're going backward. They make believe that retreat is advance, loss is gain, decay is progress. The Rams front four gains more yards without the football than the backfield does with it."*

Two members of the defensive line—end Fred Dryer and

tackle Larry Brooks—had good games that day. Dryer recorded five sacks and Brooks' play against the run had been outstanding. Tommy Prothro's "big turd from Virginia State" would have an All-Pro season and Murray wrote, *"When the ball is snapped, Brooks becomes a river flood—and the guy with the ball just a bit of flotsam floating helplessly downstream like a cow on a barn roof. But this is no babbling Brooks. Defensive tackle calls for the kind of strong, silent type who guards the gang's hideout and whose only utterance is an occasional 'You want I should pinch his head off, boss?' It's a part for Mike Mazurki. Or John Matuszak.*

"Shakespeare even had a word for him when he wrote in 'As You Like It' that we find 'Tongues in trees and books in the running brooks.'

"A rookie tackle coming into the league asked if there were any shortcuts to All-Pro at the position, and was told, 'Yeah, go copy Larry Brooks—if you can.'"

In the gloomy Rams locker room, Dryer tried to downplay his performance.

Still dressed in his dirty grass-stained blue-and-gold uniform, he looked thin and tired, and was not the peppy, swaggering figure that strutted around the lunchroom in Fullerton that summer. In general, football players were the most cooperative athletes after a game because they were beat up and exhausted.

Unlike some baseball players, who would hide in the trainer's room or the shower, which were off-limits to the media, and wait until everyone had given up and left, most football players just wanted to sit with a beer or a soft drink and catch their breath. Fred slowly pulled adhesive tape off his wrists and ankles, then heaved his jersey and shoulder pads over his head and handed them to one of the Rams equipment managers. He was not as impressed with sacks as a yardstick of excellence as some of the beat writers were. "You take pride in what you do and how well you do it. It's a team game. You play for the team. But you also play for yourself," Dryer said. "You can have an excellent game and have no sacks. On the other hand, you can have a mediocre game and run into a clumsy quarterback and have sacks."

Murray wrote, *"If pass rushers kept trophies like big-game hunters, Dryer's walls would be crammed with the tusks of some of the game's prize specimens. He has knocked Roger Staubach, Fran Tarkenton, Roman Gabriel and John Unitas unceremoniously on their hip pockets.*

"The 1979 Rams highlight film will be the first one to have to be projected backward—so the team can appear to be moving forward. They can call it 'Some Like It Cold.' The saga of the game's most pregnable offense."

In late November, USC clobbered UCLA, 49-14, to clinch the Pacific 10 championship and a berth in the Rose Bowl. The Trojans thought they had the conference title sewn up two weeks earlier when they defeated the Washington Huskies, 24-17, at Seattle. But Arizona State had to forfeit its five victories because it was discovered that eight Sun Devil players did not attend a summer school class in which they were enrolled. The decision brought Washington, upset earlier by ASU, back into the Rose Bowl picture.

Charles White scored four touchdowns in the first half and USC was on cruise control at halftime, 35-0. Paul McDonald completed 17 of 23 passes for 199 yards and ran his streak of passes without an interception to 143, a conference record. The lone bright spot for UCLA was Freeman McNeil, who rushed for 120 yards. Terry Donahue, who had never been known for his optimism, said before the game, "This is the weakest UCLA team I ever had going into an SC game." It turned out he had a right to be pessimistic.

"I think we tapped a little reserve for this game," a relieved John Robinson said afterward in the boisterous USC dressing room. "People put us in a position where we have to win again. It makes us all the more focused and determined. It was wrong to get our attention like that."

Murray took a dig at the conference's decision to award Washington a win for a game it had actually lost.

"Memo to University of Washington fans: 'OK, fellas, unpack the Winnebago. Tell Aunt Harriet never mind the potato salad. Don't put away the umbrellas. Keep the galoshes handy and the scarves and the Vapo-rub in the overcoats. Get out the longjohns. Tell the folks down at Cle Elum and Puyallup you'll be down for the holidays, after all. Nobody's going anywhere, least of all to Pasadena. Sun Bowl? Who needs it? You can't even see Monty Hall in person in El Paso. Tell grandma nobody's going to get Bob Hope's autograph.

"Forget about getting on "The Price Is Right." Arizona State didn't put the Huskies in the Rose Bowl after all. The game we had to win the Bruins blew for us. See if you can get reservations at a gin mill in Ballard. Never mind getting your lumberjacks dry-cleaned. They're all right as they are for where you're going to be spending Christmas week. You can watch the Rose Parade on TV. Enjoy the rain.'

"Arizona State didn't put USC out of the Rose Bowl by mail, after all. The Bruins couldn't invalidate the injustice."

Murray finished the month with articles on Bob Lee, the Rams' backup quarterback, and receiver Ahmad Rashad of the Vikings, and then attended the Rams-Minnesota game at the Coliseum on Sunday, December 2. The Rams won in overtime, 27-21, on a fake field-goal attempt. Safety Nolan Cromwell, who was the holder, took the ball and ran around an undefended left side for a five-yard touchdown, and this win and the following week's victory over the Falcons in Atlanta were enough for Los Angeles to clinch the NFC West title, its seventh straight, even with a dubious 9-7 record.

As the writers exited down through the stands, I led Murray outside again to the dressing rooms. L.A. was back on Standard Time and although it wasn't five o'clock yet, dusk had settled over the city. Jim walked much slower than usual and I had to take smaller steps so that I wouldn't get too far in front of him. Then something happened that I'll never forget. Security officers had set up wooden barriers to keep cars from going down the entrance to the Coliseum's tunnel from Hoover Street. There was an opening between two of the barriers and I walked through it and turned back to make sure Murray was all right. But he walked straight into the sawhorse, pitched forward and was bent over it. The crossbar prevented him from falling to the ground. I grabbed his arm and pulled him back up. "Wow," he said, shaken. "I didn't see that." He adjusted his glasses and waited while he took a deep breath. The rest of the way was clear and we joined the writers in the lobby outside the locker room.

The atmosphere was tense in the Rams dressing room. Ferragamo had started at quarterback but Malavasi pulled him late in the game and replaced him with the veteran Lee. A group of writers surrounded Vince and asked him what he thought of being taken out with the game on the line, and what he thought his future was as the team's offensive leader. Ferragamo's answers were short and terse, and as he got dressed, a grim-faced Malavasi tried to talk to him but when he saw the crowd around his quarterback, he turned and left.

On the way back to Bel-Air, Murray was quiet but then said, as we pulled up to the house, that he would call me later in the week. It was obvious something wasn't right. I asked him if he was OK but he didn't answer. He walked tentatively from the car to the open front door where Gerry stood. He went inside the house and the door closed.

Two days later, Bill Shirley announced to the sports staff that Jim would have cataract surgery on his right eye. The cataract was "ripe," and he was willing to take the risk of removal, even though it could cause the retina to detach. He was completely blind and he felt he had nothing to lose. On December 17, the day after the Rams played their last game in the Coliseum, a fitting loss to the lowly New Orleans Saints, 29-14, before a crowd of barely 50,000, doctors removed the cataract using a procedure called the "Kellman phacoemulsification technique." It was developed by Dr. Richard Kellman, a surgical procedure where a supersonic drill liquefied and pulverized the cataract without disturbing the retina.

That night the doctors removed the bandages from Murray's

eye. He blinked then focused on the hospital room TV, which the day before to him had been a white spotlight, and he saw a man wearing an orange jersey with the number 7 on the front running on a grassy green field. It was Craig Morton of the Denver Broncos and the game was Monday Night Football. Murray said, "I can see."

The phone started to ring. The first call was from Reggie Jackson, a gesture of thoughtfulness and concern by the Yankees slugger that Murray never forgot. His doctors told him to rest and Jim took their advice. He said the most beautiful sight was seeing Craig Morton on television. The moment was just as special as seeing the leaves turn color in the fall or the glowing Pacific sunsets in Malibu.

He spent the weeks of Christmas and New Year's at his vacation home in Palm Desert. He and Gerry had bought a house on the Monterey Country Club earlier that year but Jim said he had only visited the place to turn on the air conditioner "so the furniture wouldn't blow up" from the heat. But when he saw it for the first time his dream of "stepping outside and teeing it up" had come true.

He wrote a column on the Rose Bowl game, which he watched on television, and covered the Bob Hope Desert Classic from the tournament's press tent.

Craig Stadler won the Hope, and the victory, his first on the PGA tour, capped a good week for USC Trojans. The football team had beaten No. 1 Ohio State in the Rose Bowl, 17-16, a comeback win before 105,526 fans that was highlighted by an 83-yard drive and Charles White's twisting touchdown dive into the end zone.

Also the basketball team ended a 10-game losing streak to UCLA at Pauley Pavilion. In a wrap-up of the golf tournament, Jim described Stadler as "the Walrus" because of his stout, 240-pound physical appearance and droopy, bushy mustache. The British press had called Stadler the Walrus a few years earlier when he played in the British Amateur, but Murray's use of the nickname brought the ex-Trojan golfer nearly instant recognition with the American golf audience.

When I heard Shirley's announcement that Jim's eyesight had

been restored, I figured that my work with him was over, that if he could see he wouldn't need someone to look up what Mickey Mantle batted in 1956 or how many home runs Willie Mays hit in the Polo Grounds, or how many times Jack Nicklaus finished second in the U.S. Open. He could type his own columns again, and see the words. The tape recorder and optical telescope could be put in a desk drawer.

In the NFL playoffs, the Rams somehow managed to first beat the Dallas Cowboys on the road, 21-19, then stop the Tampa Bay Buccaneers, 9-0, in the NFC championship game, on three field goals by Frank Corral. The team that had been booed out of Los Angeles in its last game and drubbed in the media with farewell headlines such as "Arrivederci Aroma: Rams Smell Up Coliseum," would come back to Pasadena to play the mighty Pittsburgh Steelers in Super Bowl XIV.

I was ready to continue my pursuit of a job at another paper when Murray returned from the desert the week before the game, and he asked if I could drive him to Newport Beach for the media breakfast of the NFL's showcase event. He explained that he could drive a car to the Bel-Air Market, which was down the road from his house, or over to the Duck Blind, his favorite liquor store, on San Vicente Boulevard in Brentwood, but his doctors had forbade him to drive long distances and no, there was no way he was to get behind the wheel of a car at night.

I pulled into his driveway a little before 8 a.m. and when Murray opened the front door, he looked at me and said, "Scheib, you're a white man."

We arrived an hour later at the NFL's headquarters on Fashion Island. It was a nice change to have Murray walk in front of me. I had to hold back from opening the door for him. We got our credentials and a briefcase that, like in the World Series, included statistics, media guides, pencils, a notebook and the all-important Super Bowl pin. The NFL had the breakfast timed to the minute. Murray wrote, *"Super Bowl week is an American tribal rite*

168

as stylized as a South Seas fertility dance. The press descends en masse on the principal, and the hype is on in earnest."

For the first half hour, the media ate a continental breakfast at tables set up in a large ballroom at the Marriott hotel. At 9:45, the league's publicists brought in Coach Chuck Noll and players from the Steelers' first-string offense and defense. The writers got up from their chairs and let the players sit down at the tables. I was taken aback when I saw the Pittsburgh offensive linemen. I expected the blockers for Terry Bradshaw, Franco Harris and Rocky Bleier to be behemoths, Supermen shoulder to shoulder who blocked out the sun, ready to knock down anyone who got in their way. After all, these were the three-time Super Bowl champions. But they weren't.

The members of the offensive line, similar in size to their leader, center Mike Webster, were all about 6 feet tall and weighed about 245 pounds, short and wide, like soft drink machines. Steve Courson, Sam Davis, Randy Grossman, Gerry Mullins, Jan Kolb and Ted Petersen were slight by today's linemen standards, but quickness and strength offset their lack of size. When Bradshaw came into the room, a herd of writers, television reporters and cameramen tramped over to his table. I remarked to Jim that it was funny to watch the group, some of whom stumbled and tripped over chairs to get to Bradshaw. But Murray said sharply, "Are you kidding, a lot of these people are on deadline."

Murray joined the crowd, which had gathered four deep around the Steelers' All-Pro quarterback. A photographer for *Time* shot pictures for a story on the frenzied atmosphere of Super Bowl week, and a photo of the press at Bradshaw's table that included Murray and me ran in the magazine the following week.

Jim concentrated on the Steelers because he had written about many of the Rams' players during the season. He interviewed Jack Lambert and Franco Harris, and of Lambert, the intimidating middle linebacker who played without his dental bridge of front teeth, he wrote, *"The first time you see Jack Lambert, you're tempted to ask what he did with the fangs. Is that really tomato*

169

juice he's drinking or something he bit out of the neck of Earl Campbell? Was his coffin comfortable last night and what time does he turn into a wolf. The pro from Pittsburgh, Transylvania. If hair starts growing out of his face, get a mirror, or get out.

"*All middle linebackers are a little crazy, but Jack Lambert is the Dracula of the lot. Bela Lugosi gets the part. Karloff in cleats. Lambert didn't come out of a college. He escaped from a laboratory. Lambert is the NFL's resident Jack the Ripper. A girl in a London fog had a better chance with the original than a guy carrying a football has with the Pittsburgh counterpart in the neutral zone.*"

The next morning we were back for the Rams' players and a lot of attention went to quarterback Vince Ferragamo and defensive end Jack Youngblood, who would attempt to play in the Super Bowl with a broken leg. Youngblood sustained a hairline fracture during the playoffs and some wondered if the pain wouldn't be too much just to stand up, never mind the continuous pounding he would endure chasing into the Steelers backfield. "I can stand anything for three hours," was Youngblood's response.

Ray Malavasi named Ferragamo as the Rams' starter even though the coach had pulled him from the San Francisco and Minnesota games. Since he had taken over for Pat Haden, the team had won seven games. Before that, the Rams' record was 4-5. Ferragamo's strong passing arm played a large part in the turnaround and it also boosted Malavasi's confidence in him. Ferragamo, at 25, would be the second-youngest quarterback to start a Super Bowl game. Joe Namath was a month younger when he led the 18½-point underdog New York Jets past the Baltimore Colts in Super Bowl III. When asked about his youth and inexperience and how he was going to attack Mean Joe Greene, L.C. Greenwood and Pittsburgh's famous Steel Curtain defense, Ferragamo, sounding a bit like the brazen Namath, scoffed, "It doesn't mean anything. I feel I deserve to be where I'm at; that the Rams do too, and that we're ready to play this game. I couldn't care less if I'm the youngest Super Bowl quarterback or the oldest."

The next day, Thursday, January 17, Jim was notified that he had been named Sportswriter of the Year by the National Sportscasters and Sportswriters Association, an amazing honor considering his handicap and that he worked only half the year.

It was the fourteenth time that the organization had given him the award, another plaque for the family room wall, and it made me feel especially good to think that my work might have helped him get the recognition. The award would be presented to him, and also to Dick Enberg for top sportscaster, in a ceremony that March at Salisbury, North Carolina. What a difference a year had made.

On Sunday, Murray's advance column for the Super Bowl was on the Steelers' Harris: *"He looks like what you imagine King Solomon looked like. Or one of the Three Wise Men. Put him on a camel with a jar of gold, frankincense and myrrh and you've got a live Nativity scene. Michelangelo would rush for a chisel and slab of marble if he got a look at him.*

"The face is very Old Testament, and needs a crown on it. The eyes are black and piercing. The hair and beard are midnight black. But the skin is the color of cafe au lait. The teeth are straight and white, right out of a toothpaste ad. Maybe St. Paul looked like this. Or King Herod. Any member of the Sanhedrinn. DaVinci would use him as a model for The Last Supper. Any Shakespearean troupe would cast him immediately as Othello.

"The majestic countenance belongs not to a member of the cast at Oberammergau but to a mere football player. Well, not a 'mere' football player. He is the best player in the game. The difference.

"Franco Harris could be the best there ever was at running the football. He's no worse than second. Red Grange was the Galloping Ghost, but this is a runaway beer truck going down the Grapevine without brakes. You stop Harris, you stop the Pittsburgh Steelers. That simple. Every year he doesn't show up with cracked ribs, Pittsburgh wins the Super Bowl. You could look it up."

In the Rose Bowl press box before the game, a stream of writers stopped by Jim to congratulate him on his award and the successful cataract surgery.

171

Many of them had been at the World Series and the look on his face said it all, that he was glad to see whom he was talking to. Also, it was touching to see the younger reporters from the smaller papers tentatively approach Murray to introduce themselves. He had time for all of them.

Super Bowl XIV was expected to be a mismatch; the Steelers were 11½-point favorites on the Las Vegas line. The Pittsburgh fans streamed into the old stadium and waved their yellow-and-black Terrible Towels in anticipation of a rout. But the game turned out to be anything but. The Rams matched the Steelers' toughness and had the lead after three quarters, 19-17. When the third quarter ended, the Rams' offensive line did something I had never seen before in a football game. As the teams switched sides for the fourth quarter, Ken Iman, Jackie Slater, Doug France, Dennis Harrah and Kent Hill sprinted about 40 yards to where the referee had placed the ball, and it sent the Steelers a clear message: The Rams weren't going away.

The defense, led by Jack Reynolds, had stuffed the Pittsburgh running game, just 84 yards on the ground for Harris and Bleier. Bradshaw looked across the line of scrimmage and not only did he know the Rams had great players, he also knew they had Bud Carson, a former Steelers assistant coach who knew what Pittsburgh was going to do. Lynn Swann had to leave the game with a concussion, so, in near desperation, Bradshaw went to the air with deep passes to his other wide receiver, John Stallworth, and it paid off.

Bradshaw called "60 prevent slot, hook and go," a pass play that had been put into the Steelers' offensive repertoire the week before but hadn't worked particularly well during practice. He caught the Rams defensive secondary in a coverage mixup and hit Stallworth for a 73-yard touchdown.

After Ferragamo was intercepted by Jack Lambert in Pittsburgh territory, Bradshaw called the play again, and he connected with Stallworth on a 45-yard pass that set up Pittsburgh's last touchdown. The Steelers escaped with their fourth world championship of the 1970s, 31-19.

As the Steelers celebrated, the Rams held their heads high. "Nobody in this locker room is bitter," said Fred Dryer. "Nobody's sour. We played the hell out of those guys. I guarantee those suckers are sore too." Tackle Doug France slumped in front of his locker. "This is the tiredest I've ever been after a football game," he said. "I'm actually wore out. It was a helluva game, wasn't it?"

Murray stayed in the press box after the game and filed his column. He wrote on his portable typewriter, *"The outcome was as predictable as San Diego weather. Pittsburgh Steelers always win Super Bowl games. They're getting monotonous. But they must have thought somebody else showed up in Ram uniforms.*

"These were no Hollywood sissies, no collage of profiles, no rhinestone cowboys, no Sunset-and-Vine lilacs waiting for their big break in pictures, no guys bucking for a screen test. The Rams didn't show up with mirrors or makeup men, they were a scratching, scrambling, stubborn, socking team of alley fighters, swarmers spoiling for a scrap."

When Jim was done, he quietly packed up his typewriter and put his notes in his briefcase and we headed out of the Arroyo Seco to the Ventura Freeway and on to Bel-Air. We would return to the Rose Bowl again, for UCLA football games, an interview with Stanford's John Elway, and for Super Bowl XVII in 1983 between the Washington Redskins and Miami Dolphins. But Murray didn't need my assistance the way he did when he couldn't see.

However, at that time, the sports department would undergo a significant change in management. Bill Shirley was reassigned to a writing position and Bill Dwyre from Wisconsin was hired as sports editor.

Dwyre had come from Milwaukee to take the position of assistant sports editor, which had been Chuck Garrity's job. Garrity had been wooed by the NFL to be the managing editor of its *Game Day* magazine, a lucrative position that he accepted. With Shirley now a national sports correspondent, Dwyre suddenly found himself not on the desk as the night news editor, but head of the department.

Dwyre gradually moved me back to the copy desk fulltime and also gave me a monthly writing assignment. I helped compile the Day in Sports pages with Avrum Dansky and also wrote a column on offbeat sports, two positions that I was grateful for.

When I had to work in the office and couldn't drive Murray, he would get rides from other staff members, including Pete Thomas and Mal Florence. As Dwyre prepared for the department's coverage of the 1984 Summer Olympic Games in Los Angeles, my time with Jim came to an end.

A friend once asked what I got out of working with Murray. My answer was that I certainly learned more about journalism and the newspaper business, especially from the standpoint of a writer working on deadline. I had the good fortune of spending many summer evenings at baseball games and got to meet the players, some of whom were the greats of the game. I helped cover a World Series that turned out to be one of the best ever. And I found out the hard way that it's not easy to read out loud.

It amazed me how easily the doors of the sports world opened for Jim.

During the week of the 1983 Super Bowl, I had driven him to the Washington Redskins' media lunch at the Westin Hotel in Costa Mesa. Afterward, he said he wanted to see Jack Kent Cooke. Cooke, who owned the Redskins, hadn't attended the lunch. He was in the hotel's penthouse suite and had become somewhat of a recluse with the press. But Murray called him on the hotel's house phone and Cooke gladly invited him up to his room for a lengthy visit.

When the Lakers played the Philadelphia 76ers in the NBA Finals in 1980, Jim decided at the last minute to go to one of the games at the Forum because he wanted to interview Julius Erving. The press section was overfilled with writers from around the United States, and also from other places such as Asia and South America. But despite a lack of vacancy, the Lakers PR department had a good seat for Jim near broadcaster Chick Hearn when we arrived before the game.

But the lasting gift I got out of working with Jim Murray was that I had made a friend, somebody I could call on the telephone or write a letter to and talk about a golf tournament or what was happening in the real world. I could say with admiration that I knew Jim Murray.

I drove up the road to Bellagio Terrace and then down to the house on the left at the end of the cul-de-sac. The traffic had been light from Pasadena and we had made good time, about a 35-minute drive. It wasn't quite ten o'clock.

I parked the car in the driveway and Gerry waited at the front door. Murray got out and walked toward her. She waved and said, "Thanks, John, for taking care of my husband." I waved back and said, "Good night." For me, it had been an honor and a privilege.